PRAISE FOR
FIND THE SEEKER!

"*Find the Seeker!* is fresh as spring grass and refreshing as a clear stream. From the very start, the teachings in this book refuse to be confined to a spiritual checklist or manual of meditative techniques. Instead, the authors again and again challenge readers to return to the vibrant truth of original nature. Going beyond optimistic self-help and nihilistic despair, Genro Xuan Lou and Clifford Stevens remind us of how wonderful it is to let go of grasping and taste the vividness of direct experience."

—Robert Meikyo Rosenbaum, *neuropsychologist and psychotherapist, Zen and Qi Gong teacher, author of* Walking the Way: 81 Zen Encounters with the Tao Te Ching, *and* Zen and the Heart of Psychotherapy.

"Here is an enthusiastic account of the Zen way that is full of the excitement of discovery after discovery. Genro has an imaginative feel for how Zen can rhyme with Western tradition. The book is designed for you to take the ride and change your heart, rather than add to your learning in the normal way. It should be issued with seat belts. Genro's insight is disarming and fun and worth experiencing."

—John Tarrant, *Zen teacher, founder and director of the Pacific Zen Institute, author of* The Light Inside the Dark *and* Bring Me the Rhinoceros.

"Let go of your ideas and read this wonderful book without expectations of what the path is really about. Genro will accompany you as a true friend."

—*Taiwa Kakunen, Zen monk at the Kakunen-Ji Temple at Wachendorf Castle, Germany and Member of the Zen Group in Villingen-Schwennigen, Germany (the entire text is in the foreword to the book).*

"Like the work I have done over many decades, this book helps people to find the true Self, be One with their Divine Nature, and be free to Be. It compassionately shows people how to turn within to uncover their own Shangri-La. It is a unique, extraordinary and extremely valuable work which I highly recommend to all spiritual seekers and those who want to find what is Eternal. *Find the Seeker!* is what is needed to begin."

—*Ihaleakala Hew Len, author of* Zero Limits, *teacher of Ho'oponopono and former Chairman Emeritus of the Foundation of I.*

"There are Buddhas and patriarchs ready to accompany serious seekers. They are independent of ideologies, do not play with a spiritual baby rattle, are free of intellectual trends and stay from fundamentalist complaining.... [T]hey are guides and guardians of the 'Gateless Gate'.... Such a person is Genro Laoshi. With his book, *Find the Seeker!*, he touches your heart."

—*Xue Feng, Abbot of the Ding Shan Monastery and Chan Master, alias Konrad von Moresbach of the Oblates of the Order of St. Benedict (the entire text is in the afterword).*

"Although these teachings are by no means new, this exceptional and unique book puts them in words which people today can understand. It is a valuable guide to jumpstart your journey away from ego-based and thought-dominated suffering to Being and pure Consciousness without the usual detours. Discard your preconceptions, and let it accompany you to unfold your true, non-dual nature."

—Reza Ketabi Pour, spiritual teacher, healer and founder of the Ketabi Center

"This book is grounded, realistic and authentic. It entices us to follow the authors on the Middle Way—not in a painful, strained and complaining manner, but lighthearted and with joy. The book turns seekers into finders, and should be read again and again."

—Fritz Maywald, management consultant, trainer and author

Find the Seeker!

Find the Seeker!

The pathless path to fulfillment and happiness

**GENRO XUAN LOU, LAOSHI
& CLIFFORD STEVENS**

Columbus, Ohio

Find The Seeker: The pathless path to fulfillment and happiness

Published by Gatekeeper Press
2167 Stringtown Rd, Suite 109
Columbus, OH 43123
www.GatekeeperPress.com

Copyright © 2018 by Genro Xuan Lou, Laoshi & Clifford Stevens

All rights reserved. Neither this book, nor any parts within it may be sold or reproduced in any form or by any electronic or mechanical means, including information storage and retrieval systems without permission in writing from the author. The only exception is by a reviewer, who may quote short excerpts in a review.

LCCN: 2017963727

ISBN: 9781619848566
eISBN: 9781619848559

Find the Seeker! The pathless path to fulfillment and happiness is an expanded, revised and updated version of *Zen-sucht nach dem Wanderer* written in German by Zen Master Genro Xuan Lou, Laoshi in 2005.

Printed in the United States of America

Cover illustration:
The circle (*ensō*) is traditionally used in Zen as a symbol for enlightenment and emptiness.

"Heaven, Earth and I live together. All things and I comprise an inseparable Oneness."

—Chuang-Tzu[1]

For this simple reason, this Oneness is dedicated to Itself, the Self dedicates to Itself this book, which comes into being from it and is encompassed in it, and is therefore unthinkable.

Dwell only in the unthinkable—in the "Suchness."

If the seeker is still seeking—and the finder has not yet been found—what is left for you to do?

It will all only be revealed when Nobody is there!

Embracing all sentient beings in love,
Genro Xuan Lou, Laoshi and Clifford Stevens, 2018

CONTENTS

Foreword xv
The Challenge To You 1
Definition 11
Getting Started 19
A Pathless Path 25
Do Not Be Afraid 35
The Ego 43
Nothing Is Everything 59
The Indescribable Mystery 67
Non-Thinking 71
Wu Wei Wu 79
The Tranquil Flow 85
The Way To Perfection 91
Without Seeking 97
Be Serene 101
Quite Simple 107
True Or Not True? 113
Panta Rhei 117
Entities 121
Dioscuri—Twin Stars 127
Transformation 133
Movement And Stillness 139
Mindfulness 143

Unity And Peace	147
Wu-Nian	151
Grace	153
Blessed Are The Poor In Spirit	157
Wisdom	161
Doubt	167
The Journey Within	177
The River Of Life	183
Vast Expanses	189
About The Ego	201
Bring Us Your Chains	203
Afterword	207
About The Authors	211
Additional Reading	213
Notes	215

FOREWORD

by Taiwa Kakunen

To Genro Laoshi,

Some time ago our paths crossed. I have had the privilege of reading your wonderful book.

I have been focusing on Buddhism and Zen for very many years, in short, with the path of life. During my travels to many faraway countries, I learned one thing. "You can only find whatever you are searching for within yourself."

I gave up my search and was ordained as a Zen monk. I arrived, namely at the beginning of a path which led me to the most distant places without my even taking one step. These places cannot be described in any book.

So when I got your book, I did not expect to read anything new. Whoever buys books today will usually be overloaded with more or less interesting stories about the topic of Zen and/or Buddhism. For centuries, all kinds of people have been writing down their thoughts about these hope-giving matters, usually derived from the knowledge obtained from other books.

So when I finally had the copy of your book in my hands, I was really surprised. It did not contain the usual sayings which have been handed down. Instead, my traveling companion Genro Laoshi stood next to me. He was an invisible friend, but one whose presence I strongly felt, who smiled at me from time to time as I trod on my path.

What I read the following evenings seemed to be a mirror of my own life. This book described part of my own path, and it was not easy to put the book down, because I wanted to know how it continued.

Many years ago, my old Chinese Zen Master Shi Deyu said to me that I had come to China with my ideas and concepts. Now I can say the same to every reader. Let go of your ideas and read this wonderful book without expectations of what the path is really about. Genro will accompany you as a true friend, as he did for me.

I do not want to get ahead of anyone and take away the wonderful realizations they can have on the path. As a wanderer, I only want to remove one tiny pebble from the path.

Life is not as it seems, and as you have experienced it so far. When the fairy tale of Santa Claus (and Father Christmas) only proved to be a nice story, some of you were sad, but the expectations of what did not exist slowly dissipated. This is similar to many other things which we consider to be real and unalterable. They are stories originating from thoughts of the past.

With a deep bow to you, and many thanks,

—Taiwa Kakunen
Zen monk at the Kakunen-Ji Temple
at Wachendorf Castle, Germany and
Member of the Zen Group
in Villingen-Schwennigen, Germany

THE CHALLENGE TO YOU

THERE IS AN endless vanity fair of seemingly life-changing books on spirituality, esotericism, religion, mysticism and meditation. They offer their own recipes for the "right" path to happiness and to reaching the Kingdom of God. They are almost as numerous as grains of sand by the sea and compete for our loyalty.

So why publish yet another such book? Why publish a book which is admittedly not a typical entertaining, wishy-washy, "feel-good" book pandering to people and offering a quick fix and precise instructions, but which challenges every fiber of your being and even risks seeming preachy and prescriptive?

Why publish a book which tells you that you ultimately do not need any teachers, sacred texts, intermediaries, gurus or any book, not even this one?

Why should you read a book of tough love, which calls upon you to let go of your thinking, logic, emotions, ego processes and your past, and asks you to unlearn many of the things you were brought up to believe in and rely upon?

And finally, why read a book which invites you to take a journey on the pathless path to the One Self (which you already are) and go through the gateless gates to hear the sound of the iron flute?

For one thing, many of us are living dysfunctional lives—as viewed from a spiritual perspective.

We often transform the path into being as we really are, that is, our true, Absolute Self (the most natural thing in the world), into an overly complicated, burdensome task.

Moreover, we delude ourselves—a fallacy unfortunately reinforced by many books and teachings—into believing that there are countless "steps" and "goals" to attain before accomplishing this, and so much we have to "learn" before we can "reach" our goal, instead of realizing that we already ARE what we seek. Many of us desperately strive and struggle just to be what we inherently are, looking for happiness elsewhere—instead of turning within to the Self.

In addition, we constantly dwell on the past or look ahead to some feared or desired future instead of abiding in the here and now, in the Oneness, the Source, Divinity, Tao or however you may name it.

We focus too often on doing, having, and achieving—in line with what we have been taught and the image we have of ourselves and others have of us—instead of on "being."

Finally, we still need so many words to motivate us to turn within despite the many teachers, masters and prophets who have showed us the way. Like a united choir of the wise men and women who have worked on the face of the Earth, they serve as signposts and facilitators enabling us to one day to embody that which is indescribable and indefinable.

We hope these tried and tested seeds will fall on fertile ground.

"Abiding" in the Self (not one's own limited self)—which comprises our real mojo—is ultimately more breathtaking, rewarding and joyful than any other pastime, activity, work or form of recreation on Earth. The pathless path—and not any travel destination, adventure or extreme sport—is the ultimate frontier.

This book has been written to compassionately accompany you on this journey, which you will come to realize you have always been on and will always be on.

We are not offering a guide to meditation or a manual on how to achieve happiness. This book provides neither a description of Eastern philosophy or religion nor a to-do list of rules. It does not try to convert you to any particular religious beliefs. Instead, it focuses on the spiritual dimension underlying all Existence—which all of us share. Absolute Being or Oneness goes beyond all conditions, conventions and confessions.

This book aims to pick you up where you are and help you reboot your spiritual search and renew your life. It will incessantly hammer away at your dependence on your ego by repeatedly driving home the point (even if you get tired of hearing it) that searching outside of your Self leads nowhere.

In other words, this is not a self-help but a Self-reliant book which will point out the way for you to BE bliss in the here-now.

Let this book unfold in and work on you to slowly reach its crescendo. Unlike a novel which you may read in a few sittings or even all at once, a good spiritual book is like a symphony that one can repeatedly listen to. Immerse yourself in it in the here-now, and allow each page to turn into a revelation or an awakening. By doing such, you will enable the book to point to the Isness and Suchness—even if your mind does not comprehend everything right away.

Such a display of patience is certainly not an easy task for many readers, especially considering our bulletin point-addicted, teaser trailer, fast-paced, self-centered and fun-loving society. In line with the motto "been there, done that," people today often equate trying out many fads and spiritual paths with making progress. Yet they are often unaware of their being enslaved under the guise of being free to choose.

The great Indian sage Ramana Maharshi put it simply, yet profoundly. He admonished us to "be as you are." This is a key message of this book. However, in our present day and age, we frequently exploit this bit of wisdom to justify even greater egoistic indulgence, self-staging and self-delusion. There are many traps on the so-called spiritual path, which unfortunately often ends up turning into a well-disguised ego trip or which continues our dependency and self-delusion. We fall prey to the lures of "individualism" and thus miss being in the Oneness.

There is nothing wrong at all with enjoying life and savoring the countless beautiful moments it has to offer. This book is not a call for asceticism or for the renunciation of pleasure. But we do ask you to stop for a moment to consider all the activities, media, high-tech gadgets, temples of consumption and leisure time possibilities offered by modern life. Ponder the connections to the Web, Facebook, Twitter, Instagram, online games, virtual reality experiences and whatever else is popular at a given moment or yet to be invented. They may all be satisfying and enjoyable. However, they are only temporary in nature—as are relationships, success and all the physical forms manifesting themselves in this material world of ours.

It may be momentarily entertaining or event riveting to see the latest movie or TV episode, to read a bestseller, to go to a travel destination which is "in," to strive to get "enough" of whatever it is we desire, or to "add value" to our lives. However, these are only illusive distractions, especially if we fail to put them in their proper context.

There is no doubt that new technologies offer many advantages. Nevertheless, one thing is certain: bliss can appear within a single moment, but not through the click of your mouse or by using an app. Absolutely nothing you "do"—no activity or effort on your part, and no outside influence or external event—can add to or take away from your inherent nature of Oneness.

The age-old pathless path, which is not a modern-day concoction or "discovery" by the authors, does not promise to miraculously eliminate all the difficulties or challenges each of us faces in the outside world. However, it can change the way we are inside, enabling us to inwardly accept what is going on, to deal with it with inner strength and serenity, to lead more fulfilled lives and most importantly, simply to be.

The materialistic, relative world is impermanent and transitory, and is thus unable to give us all the answers. Our limited intellects do not enable us to grasp absolute truth and the ultimate reality. Although it is a valuable tool, the mind cannot offer all the answers we need to deal with suffering, pain and tragedy, not to mention our mortality. We are used to the mind weaving intricate labyrinths of thought processes, mind maps and problem-solving techniques. Their weaving and employing is impelled by the futile hope of getting us further down the road.

The famous statement attributed to the Greek philosopher Socrates, "All I know is that I know nothing," points out to us that the logical mind cannot grasp the Absolute Isness. This book is not a call to arms but a plea to disarm your supposed "ego." Get rid of your crutches and regain your childlike awe and love for life!

Bliss was your original state. However, most of you have failed to live up to more than a mere fraction of your potential and currently live in a state of unawareness. If you want to rediscover what is lying under the surface, you need to unfold and unleash your own inner guru. You are also required to turn within to your innermost Self through humility, mindfulness and meditation. The age-old Zen parable, "if you meet the Buddha, kill him," clearly admonishes us not to depend on anything or anybody outside our-Selves.

People worship their egos more than all the gods, and the tyranny exerted by the ego accompanied by its never-ending story of thoughts and emotions dwarfs any kind of political tyranny known to man. Not to mention the fact that the ego is responsible for the "isms" that continue to plague humanity: egoism, individualism, fanaticism, fundamentalism, nationalism and so many more.

It is not as much a question of learning as un-learning what we have been mistakenly brought up to believe. If you continue as you have up until now, the soap opera of your life will continue to victimize you. It will play out on the screen of your life in a non-stop, never-ending showing.

We are not seeking knowledge but Self-realization. Your Self is always with you—it is always you. You can get a divorce from your partner, change jobs or travel to a faraway land, but your Self is always there, closer than your very breath. You do not have to re-invent yourself because it is all there.

The underlying message is by no means a new one. It is timeless and just as relevant for this day and age as it will be for future generations: Know Thyself and you will be free. Or to put it in other words: The Kingdom of God is within you. The Buddha Nature is (in) every one of us. Knock and the door will be opened to you.[2]

We are attached to the material world of our senses and all their limitations. However, we do have the capability of emptying ourselves of our constant thoughts, worries and ego-based actions. We can abide in the nothingness and emptiness, which, contrary to logic, is actually the all-encompassing Allness and fullness.

The seeming paradox is that you can only be somebody if you are Nobody. The Divine can only enter if Nobody is there, as will be explained later. The freedom-craving individualist has yet to realize that he or she is not in control. The challenge is to fully let go. We cannot live Life, but we can abide in Oneness and allow Life to live us.

It is our challenge to reject the limited "self" which thinks it has a life of its own, and the false belief in duality as well. As this book explains, there is really no individual "I," "my" or "mine." There is no self-hood apart from the One Self, God, One Mind. Another Indian sage, Sri Nisargadatta Maharaj, states: "The real you is timeless and beyond birth and death."[3]

We can be filled to the brim with Beingness. There is an alternative to being victimized by our person-alities, to being caught up in the endless rollercoaster rides of life's ups and downs, and that is becoming more aware, becoming mindful of the present moment. We are to realize that we are not "the thinker," as Eckhart Tolle so convincingly shows us.[4] We have the ability to rest in what he calls "the eternal present." We are capable of doing what we think we need or want to do, and to do such without being attached to, identifying with and imprisoned by all of this.

Nobody else can go down this path for us, even though many people today cling to the "guidance" supposedly offered by such celebrities or "teachers." This book countervails the objectives of many longstanding spiritual teachings. In turn, these have a vested interest in keeping people dependent. They achieve this by focusing on such "superficial" manifestations of spirituality as their places of worship, rituals and ceremonies—instead of concentrating upon the inner presence within us. Such teachers are interested in ensuring that the status quo of the "establishment" is not disturbed.

If the soul is not aware of its being free and liberated, any action or letting go will be in vain. Release the Scrooge-like chains that imprison you into believing you are anything less than pure, unconditional, Absolute Being. What you already are is much more than what you can ever make of yourself by exerting yourself, by accumulating a critical mass of personality, experiences and knowledge. And once you've "crossed the river," you can dispense with the raft containing all your burdens, false belief in duality, ego-based misconceptions and the supposedly "necessary" spiritual practices. You will be able to fully enjoy the lightness and bliss of Being and to live in the here-now.

This book is capable of merely giving you a hint of what awaits you. Don't simply take our word for it. The work of finding the truth will have to be "done" by you. And this work won't be "intellectual" in nature. Enticing as it may be to reflect or philosophize about truth, it can only be palpably and directly experienced—by your turning within!

Drop all your thoughts, concepts, preconceptions and expectations, and begin this book with an open, unencumbered mind. There are many versions of a well-known story about a university professor who visited Zen Master Nan-in during the Meiji era in Japan[5] and was invited to drink a cup of tea. The Zen Master poured tea until the professor's cup was full, and then kept on pouring until the tea was all over the table and on the floor. The professor beseeched him to stop because the cup was already full. Nan-in replied, "Your mind is like this teacup. You are so full of your own opinions, knowledge and prejudices that nothing more can be added. Empty your mind so that you can learn something new."

Who is the person reading this book? Who is the seeker, the one searching for happiness, fulfillment and/or enlightenment? Why do you want to know this?

Join us and stroll along the pathless path that you have

always been on. Stop to linger by the wayside as you begin your journey within, this inner pilgrimage to that which you embody. Live life as it really is—as light as a feather. Embrace and be the Infinite Self that you already are. Let this book begin to awaken you to your true nature.

DEFINITION

"Ordinary people or sages are both only names. Their inner nature is not different. Names are only symbols for what does not exist in reality!"

—Ta-Mo[6]

LIFE ITSELF IS the real spiritual practice, and this means only one thing: Being. Being is not taking action to have or to get something, and can only be a state of "non-practicing." Beingness is the path to our center, our Self. This "being in the center" is what comprises meditation and abiding in the Oneness.

Revered Masters from all religions are called upon to help us be aware of, connect back to, and reside in the center of our being. This reconnection comprises the essence of the Latin word "religare," which is considered to be the basis of the word "religion." Displaying untiring and endless compassion, these Masters endeavor in their unique manner to make the truth accessible to people. The Masters use words, gestures, stories and meditation techniques to help us gain this access.

This book will often refer to the major spiritual teachers of life by their names. But what's in a name? Names are nothing more than hollow shells. Their importance pales when being compared to the significance of what these people have to teach us—provided that we manage to truly understand their messages. It is precisely these teachers, these fully enlightened human beings who have the capability of serving as signposts and as exemplifiers of the grace that we need to make our way down the path. These teachers are the ones who have attained the undivided, non-dual consciousness that puts them far beyond the average individual. The high level of awareness that they have attained manifests itself in their ways of living, goodness, love and compassion. We can only hope that their wisdom bears fruit.

Due to our need for definitions to satisfy and feed our minds, we turn to one Master who defined meditation in a way that provides us with a strong inkling of what is meant:

Osho says: "When mind knows, we call it knowledge. When heart knows, we call it love. And when Being knows, we call it meditation."[7]

You will certainly understand the first part, because the mind knows what we experience when we think we understand something. When we have understood something, we call it knowledge. Then it is placed in the archive of our consciousness, in a manner similar to a computer's storage of data on a hard disk. You may refer to this storage as "consciousness,"[8] or "memory." We are capable of drawing upon the ensuing wealth of experience whenever or however we want. We are well acquainted with the process. As such, it does not require any further explanation.

Now let's turn to what the Master describes as being what the heart realizes. We sometimes refer to this as "love." This is much more difficult to define, because we cannot see love, nor can we mold, think, buy or retain it. We cannot even come close to describing it.

Definition

There are so many books and statements about love and by famous poets, wise philosophers and prominent individuals. Studying these makes you aware of the vast size of the iceberg of our feelings and emotions lying beneath the surface of the water. This "iceberg" has ample space for contradictory moods. Love cannot be empirically comprehended by the mind. Nor does a formula exist to categorize it. Love is not capable of being "pigeonholed."

Love is akin to the fine arts. You can only "grasp" them with your heart. If we wanted to define love, any attempt to do so would be doomed to fail. Can you precisely specify what a symphony composed by Mozart actually is? We can only lend a voice to it, and great artists can make us feel what they are trying to express.

Please turn your attention to the last part of Osho's definition. Now try to see it in your mind's eye. This will make it easier for you to perceive the great subtlety of "realizing with your entire being."

Osho says, "Only when your entire being is imbued, words are no longer sufficient and feelings cannot grasp and embrace it, will the truth reveal itself through your inner tranquility, and peace and serenity pervades you. You see yourself as godlike, and thus you have returned to the center of your being. You are no longer separate, and there is only Being."

Adam and Eve were expelled from the Garden of Eden (paradise or the enlightened state of awareness) and its Oneness of all Beingness upon Eve's plucking the first emotions that our minds could perceive from the Tree of Knowledge.[9] This caused the emergence of the discursive thought and the dualistic thinking that emphasized their perceived separation from God.

It is interesting to note that Japanese people familiar with the Bible believe paradise is not something which is eternally irretrievable. Instead, they believe that you instantaneously return to paradise upon realizing that your consciousness has retained its original pureness, that it is undivided. This realization is brought about by humility. What this means is that you were never irreversibly expelled. You caused your expulsion, and you thus have the capability to reverse the first or Original Sin.

The Chan and Zen Masters of the East demand of us to "show your true face before there was a father or mother" or to "see your Original Face."[10] In other words, they call upon us to seek and find the undivided, unconditional and inviolable Being. This is our inherent nature. It is completely open and connected to all and everything. To do such, we have to learn to recognize the shadows and the blindness that they give rise to.

Should we manage to do so, the ego, which has lowered itself onto us like a huge sponge, can be recognized for what it is: an illusion and a figment of our imagination. Our paying homage to the ego enables it to disarm our capability for understanding and for Self-realization!

The mind does provide us with advantages and disadvantages. This may seem to be a trivial or mundane statement, but it is easy to understand. This is because most people's minds exist in a state of duality. The mind cannot help noting that there is Yin and Yang, that they accompany us, that they govern us and our actions. The only way for us to escape this duality is for us to find and go down the pathless path. To that end, the Master asks the question:

"If all discursive things ultimately go back to the One, where does the One go back to?"

This important koan[11] will leave you standing there feeling as if you had a glowing ball of energy or light in your stomach.[12] A koan is not to be solved logically by the rational mind. Should you care to do such, you can spend the coming years attempting to figure this one out. We promise to bow down to you in respect should you ever reach the point at which the meaning of this koan is revealed to you. Although the path is indescribable, one can wander on it. Following the pathless path enables us to transcend a route for growth that people are prone to judge as being "good" or "bad."

Your intellect does not possess the capability required to figure out the koan for you. It was never conceived for this purpose. To provide an analogy, you would be equally incapable of measuring the size of a table by using such a high precision, technically advanced device as a blood pressure monitor, for the simple reason that the latter wasn't designed to fulfill this specific task.

The purpose of the existence of your mind is to enable you to use it to transform your experience and knowledge into wisdom. Your mind places what you have learned at your disposal. This allows you to store, re-use and draw upon it whenever you like. However, the mind has another proclivity: it exploits your experiences to distract you from living in the present moment.

This is because of your mind's propensity to contemplate and dwell on everything imaginable, also encompassing the thoughts behind your thoughts—instead of its being in the here and now. It should be noted that the mind possesses such useful skills as the ability to ward off harm by anticipating and planning. However, it also drags along a burdensome and heavy backpack whose size varies depending on the individual. This "backpack" is full of our experiences of the past and the judgments—seemingly good or bad—that we have pronounced on them.

The mind also contains misgivings, apprehensions, fears, beliefs, visions and fantasies as well as sensible ideas and helpful hopes. On the one hand, the mind's workings are the key to our survival. On the other hand, they thwart our ability to live well and fully. This impairment arises from the mind's tendency to interpret things in a self-destructive manner. In fact, this self-destructiveness can be so strong that it causes us to doubt everything and ourselves, even to the point of our wanting to die.

When you finally realize that neither your mind nor your heart has the capability of leading you to your original Being and your Self, you will realize that only grace has this ability. The failure of a person to reconnect to his inner Self means that meditation may sooner or later be needed to help her or him live in harmony with herself or himself.[13]

When you are One with everything, you will attain the point of being able to draw your strength from the depths of your roots, to allow the energy to flow freely in you, and to be able to release this energy after it has stimulated and inspired you. In this case, your energy gates are wide open. This situation is akin to electricity, which has to be able to flow without experiencing any resistance in order to be usable.

The parables found in Buddhism as well as the practice of yoga in India serve as guideposts that show us the way in which we have to go. For example, Buddhism makes use of the symbol of the lotus flower rooted in mud. The lotus flower, one of the most beautiful in the world, derives its strength from the morass lying underneath it. This tapping of the strength enables the flower to sprout the most stunning blossoms on the surface. The blossoms appear to be bathed in heavenly light.

Another well-known symbol is the science of alchemy, which is based upon the practice of transformation. The purpose of alchemy is to produce gold. In turn, gold has been the symbol of the universal life force in Chinese mythology for thousands of years. Alchemy is also associated with self-transformation and the rescuing of the soul.

> "If the branches of a tree want to rise as far up as heaven, the roots have to extend down into the Earth."

From the Chinese perspective, Heaven and Earth are the two poles between which a human being lives and experiences her or his own development. We are rooted in the Earth but stand upright towards heaven. This situation is similar to that of the lotus flower, which takes root in the mud, but then blossoms as it reaches out towards the light.

The true meaning of religion is to reconnect us to our original, primordial Being. Masters who were divinely blessed in realizing the truth have shown us the path to take enabling us to reconnect.

Finally, we come to the third part of Osho's definition. The path to our own Self can be found by realizing our own Being, which is this book's focus.

In the drama of your own life, you do more than just play the main role with which you have identified up until now. You are also the author of the play—and the director as well. You are the one determining who says what, and when and how. You are also in control of the assigned roles, the casting and performance, the point in time the actor enters or departs from the stage, and how each person plays his part.

Consider yourself to be both prompter in the theater and one of the actors. Prize being able to see yourself as a member of the audience watching this play, which is performed on the stage of life. Understand that you are the one who is reflecting, perceiving, and realizing this play's wonderfulness and horribleness at this very moment. Don't forget that everything is One and that you are a house undivided. You are simultaneously the observer of and the actor in the play. You are the stage, the play and the player. It is truly your very own show.

The realization of being in the moment is lost as soon as you begin to recapitulate.

Every time something happens, you begin afterwards to think about what happened. Although these thoughts may sometimes be beneficial, as they can constitute the basis for "learning," they do have downsides. We frequently end up getting entangled and ensnared in these thoughts. This causes you to no longer live in the present reality or in the here-now. That is why you should not allow yourself to be controlled and dominated by your mind. It creates all the concepts you identify with.

Here is a point to be considered. No other life except for the life you have right now is perceptible to you at this moment. On the pathless path, you can learn to "know yourself." This will enable you to take that marvelous but perhaps difficult step of accepting life as it is, and of accepting yourself as you are. In turn, this will allow you to enjoy and love life, to plunge into its depths, and to explore the unlimited possibilities open to you as the divine being that you are.

The lights of pure, genuine truth illuminate this path in such a merciful and soothing manner as we go about penetrating the depths of our inner being. The journey along the pathless path may well be accompanied by physical and emotional anguish as well as mental torment. Isn't this comforting to know?

> **"The thoughts and concepts arising from thinking come from the separation of the ego and nature, and are thus subject to judgments. However, the path is free from standards, distinctions and desires."**
> —Ta-Mo

GETTING STARTED

"You wanderer on the path! There is no path, only wandering."

—Francis of Assisi

People harbor a longing to discover their inner wanderer. This means that they long to get to know their own Self, their original state, which existed before there was a father or mother. That is why many of us get involved in the lifelong search for God, Divinity, Tao, Primordial Being, the "Original Face" or whatever name we give it.

In this process, the consciousness in us seeks It-Self. Let us take a very short detour to give you a bit of background on this book, which is based on our experiences with Zen. It is a path enabling people to live without being judgmental. Zen is all-encompassing. It embraces life and death and all seeming opposites and contradictions. Zen excludes nothing and serves as an unconventional companion for us. It goes beyond all established religions.

One thing is important to say at the outset: the ultimate truth cannot be put into words. How can one describe the Absolute in relative terms? As one Zen Master put it, trying to pin down or define the all-encompassing Oneness is like trying to hammer a nail in the open sky.

As wanderers, we usually pose the question, "why?" when phenomena are perceived. Zen lovingly yet determinedly throws us back onto our Selves, and the ultimate source of what is perceived. Zen accordingly asks, rather, "who?" This is the perceiver of everything that can be perceived, which is usually called the "10,000 Things."[14] The seeker who seeks is actually that which is being sought!

Experiencing the Oneness of all Existence, which Christians have often referred to as the "mystical marriage," unites the wandering, the wanderer and the path. It is all One. The Oneness can be lived, embodied and practiced. This enables us to boldly go down the pathless path and to pass through the gateless gate. This state is what spiritual masters throughout the ages have termed "enlightenment."

In this state, we simply stand back and observe the activity of grace, of spiritual practice and of our Being, whenever and wherever this occurs. This takes the place of our being ensnared in the soap operas of our lives, which we mistakenly think is the ultimate reality.

We come closer to the absolute One, the I AM THAT I AM[15] from which all things originate. We ask: "If there is only One, where does this One return to?" Time and again, this question arouses in us a desire for a solution that will satisfy our innermost longings.

People view matters in a variety of ways. They have a variety of imaginings of the nature of truth, and live their varying dreams of life in this world. Dreaming is what unites all of us, which means we are neither alone nor isolated. All of us are inseparably linked in the One.

Zen seeks the perceiver, without whom perception would not exist in the first place. Zen also seeks what Is, the basis for all appearances. It leads us through the "Such-ness" of all Being to our-Selves, and ultimately to the one Self.

Getting Started

The truth is completely here. It can only be experienced in the here and now. Trying to pin it down is impossible.

This good news was propagated by the founders of religions. It was then written down—to convey the news to subsequent generations—by the authors of the Bible, Bhagavad Gita and other scriptures. However, the authors have not achieved what they originally aspired to because many of their statements have been wrongly interpreted. Moreover, their teachings have been transformed into dogmas, whose formulations have become more important than the essence of what the Masters taught over the ages. People mistakenly confuse the "fingers" pointing to the moon (words, concepts, scriptures, rituals) for the moon itself (i.e. pure awareness of the Oneness, the Tao, Being etc.).

The unfortunate result of this transformation is that very many people believe that the key precondition for the entering of the Kingdom of God is the strict compliance with the moral codes, rules and laws of their particular religion.

This brings us to ponder three key questions:

Have we really been hopelessly and helplessly inserted into the universe to suffer amidst a harsh, merciless Existence? Or are we part and parcel of the Oneness?

Are we forced to fanatically cling to religious precepts and rules because we would be disoriented otherwise?

Do we consider ourselves unworthy of entering the Kingdom of God unless we go through countless steps, practices, rituals and rites?

Dogmatically held beliefs separate us. The longing for truth and the search for the Ultimate unites us and enables us to seek together.

The dangers of dogma and fundamentalism are demonstrated by the plethora of religious wars in both the past and present, by the atrocities human beings have committed in the name of God, and by the persecution of people holding other beliefs.

So let us put aside our doubts. Let us start seeking so that we will finally realize that the truth itself would appear to be well concealed—in us.

How long did I, Genro, drag myself around the world on my search! Only after a very memorable and powerful experience did a small group to which I belonged have the privilege of "seeing the light." When we demanded a response to the ultimate questions, the response of our Master was to show us tough love. This was brutally but compassionately and effectively administered. It forced us to turn inwardly to our own Self.

We besieged and pestered our Master. We asked him to explain the truth to us and to finally give us the answers that we so desperately wanted. His response was merely to have us return to sitting in Zazen, the meditation posture of Zen Buddhism, for seemingly never-ending periods of time. This caused us to reach the point where we couldn't sit any longer, as the pain had become unbearable.

So one day we finally went to speak to him. We were distressed. We were suffering from self-imposed mental anguish. We were also experiencing the healing pressure of observing our own consciousness. The questions arose: "Couldn't we have done the same thing at home in the West? Couldn't we have sat down on the floor in our homes and dealt with our own thoughts there? Couldn't we have ended up by finally releasing them, thus discovering our inner quietue? Wouldn't this have been just as effective as sitting here in a remote monastery, without the need for so much instruction?" In response, the Master smiled and answered: "It's already working!"

You cannot increase or improve upon your Buddha Nature, no matter how far you travel, no matter wherever you go on this planet or whatever you do. "It" is completely with you and in you. There is no far-away divine reality that you have to seek or attain because this "It" is already present in you.

"It" is you.

"It" is with you wherever you go, no matter where you may go to try to escape despair, worry and fear, no matter where your pursuit of "added value" may take you. Pursuing this path will enable you to find "It" anywhere and everywhere.

This book relates "mystic seeds"—intensive experiences and insights. Many of these stem from sources which are no longer accessible, whereas others are those that were experienced first-hand. The important thing to remember is that all of us—we and you—have been blessed with the grace to deeply absorb these mystic seeds. We are in fact fertile ground for them.

This openness is concealed in your Self, so do not go looking for it elsewhere. When doing such, please remember the timeless words of the Oracle of Delphi in Greece. This wisdom forms part of our spiritual tradition. The Oracle's words are clear and unequivocal. They touch a sensitive spot in us:

"Know Thyself—Know Thy Self!"

You may well think: "That's easier said than done!" The explanation as to why most of us cannot manage to accomplish it immediately is because our senses have been rendered incapable of perceiving, and because much has been suppressed or swept under the carpet.

However, your dwelling in unconsciousness, though ramifying upon the entire cosmos, passes, dissolves and disappears into nothingness once your mind achieves the calmness and tranquility ensuing from its being in the here-now and being allowed to rest. The virtues of rest should be apparent to you at this very moment. While reading this book, you are no doubt resting your legs (because we assume that you have sat down somewhere to read it in peace).

Should you wish to get involved with people whom others may consider to be "out of their minds," who are no longer where they once were, then come and join us. (The phrase "out of your mind" precisely expresses what we are striving to achieve—to get you away from the dominance of your mind.) Learn firsthand what even this book cannot express. Once you have understood this, it will cause you to disregard or throw into the fire every book that claims to precisely describe enlightenment, the pathless path or the ultimate truth—even this one!

Let's suppose you want to leave the room in which you are sitting and writing. The first step will have to be made in the very same room. Similarly, if you are looking for a way to transcend your mind and to quiet your thinking, your mind is the initial instrument you need to understand, to the extent that this is possible. The first step towards achieving this relies on words, terms, synonyms and illustrations. As you may be able to already gather, all this has absolutely nothing to do with the truth, not in the slightest.

Let's get on with it!

A PATHLESS PATH

Let us take a few steps together down the pathless path. The wheel has already been invented, which makes it unnecessary to reinvent. By the same token, you can be spared the painful experience—by taking a guide—of repeatedly making your way down paths that are unknown to you and are destined to be difficult. For the time being, take a guide who will wander along the path with you and help you to move ahead courageously.

Be aware that this guide can only convey something to you if she or he is alert and mindful. Pay attention to what she or he does and how she or he does it, how she or he speaks and looks, and whether she or he is enlightened.

Don't fall into the trap of following someone who is himself misguided. Be cautious if you confront a false prophet or guru. There are a large number of them in the world, and they do not know what they are doing. Even worse, they have the alcoholic's propensity for getting their buddies to drink with them, so that they too will succumb to this addiction. Their success in doing such will cause others to share their disorientation and obscured vision.

Finding a truly enlightened Master or a teacher—one capable of giving you advice and pointers—is a difficult matter. A capable guide is one who gives you, in a timely manner, the opportunity to be thrown back upon your-Self. The results of guiding your search for the wanderer could and should be to uncover the Master in you, to follow, listen to and trust it—without being dependent on anyone else.

Don't misjudge the situation and mistakenly believe that the realization of the potential within you is far away—elsewhere in time and place or in some distant future. The opposite is true. Be assured that your innermost being is always there, always close by for you and always accessible. You are and will always be eternal!

"The Kingdom of God is within you."

If this statement is really true, is there anything outside of you limited by time and space?

To answer this question, please allow yourself to be grabbed by the nose and have it pulled and twisted until you scream in pain, as a few Zen Masters are known to have done! Who is the one spontaneously crying out from the bottom of your very being? Who is the one who flinches and winces upon the thunder's clapping after the lightning strikes? Who is the one making sure you slam on the car brakes, thus preventing you from running over the cyclist crossing on your right?

Admit that all this happens without having to think twice, without you pondering it. This intuitive ability to respond is you! If you find your real Self, you can say, "I AM THAT I AM." This means that you are now able to understand all the Masters who "lock eyebrows" with you.[16] This going "face-to-face" is what the Chan Masters call the "great understanding." It is a field of perception instilled in our mind's eye. In it, everything is interwoven and comprises one Mind. This enables you to realize that both the Kingdom of God and all space and all time lie within you. That is what you are, have always been and will always be. We dream of seeking and finding such a paradise as the legendary Shangri-La.[17] In fact, this paradise lies inside you, the only place you can find it.

You no longer have to feel separated from the world. You no longer have to feel as if you were cast away on a deserted island, isolated from everything. In reality you ARE all of Existence. You are inseparable from the Oneness because you originate from the One. Or show me a single place where God isn't present?

Your trust in us is required to agree to allow us to accompany you down your path. Should you care to do so, take our hand when wandering on the pathless path. However, when doing such, you will have to experience the path all by yourself. The underlying reason is that there is nobody outside of you, as everything is One Being. We will simply walk with you on this path as long as you continue to make distinctions and insist on believing in duality.

What you are doing at this very moment and what your life is all about—your friends, acquaintances, the work you do, how you spend your free time and all your activities—constitute this part of the journey on the pathless path. There is nowhere you have to go, nothing you have to begin with, and nowhere that you have to begin. Should you choose to wander with us, you will soon realize that you are already on the path and have always been on it. There is nothing else you could have done except to continue wandering.

> "The path is right beneath your feet," under you.[18]

You have never been on another path. You have chosen this path and can spare yourself a lot of needless worrying about whether or not your decision will cause you to miss the chance of going down another path.

Doesn't the perfection of Being also include imperfection, and thus all possible and impossible paths?

Isn't it absolutely marvelous to know that there is nobody on this path to disturb you and interfere with you? Only violence has the potential to deter you from peacefully and serenely wandering on this path.

All self-inflicted violence is actually the result of your own unawareness.

In Japan, it is said that there is only one sin, and that is to act unknowingly. Accordingly, the belief is widespread in the country that the punishment for committing a sin will not come sometime in the future, in some future hell or purgatory. What will be punished much sooner is acting mindlessly!

We have occasions to observe this in our daily lives. One example is when you work mindlessly and injure yourself in the process. In this case, you immediately bear the consequences of your lack of attentiveness. Another example is the absent-minded professor peeling potatoes but thinking about seemingly "important" problems. As a result, he is completely unmindful and careless. He cuts his finger, and his pain represents an instant punishment for his mindless behavior.

If we need it, the grace of pain and suffering enables us to awaken.

We can awaken to the place—the Allness, the Oneness—where we have not yet learned to linger and dwell. This is a place where we are not attached to the occurrences of the outside world. Most of us do not yet experience the magnificent gift of seeing when our eyes are whole. We do not even sense well-being when we are free from pain.

Our own suffering and the suffering of others summon us to engage in Self-reflection. This helps us view our inmost Being. We live in a troubled world. Has it ever been any different? Arising from everything from natural catastrophes, death and disease to war, poverty, famine and much more—not to mention what we inflict on ourselves—suffering prods us to explore the meaning of life more deeply. You will recognize the path once you have been awakened and have been made aware by suffering.

We can only become meditative—centered in the Self—by being mindful.

This is what one Chinese Master meant when he taught his pupils that "mindfulness is the path to meditation." Responding to the request placed by his followers for other tips on how to live consciously, the Master reaffirmed his first answer by repeating the word: "mindfulness." And when his pupils pressured him to go on, he simply said for the third time: "mindfulness."

Mindfulness, the practice of which may take time for you to learn, means focusing your attention on the present moment (which is eternal) instead of on the past or future. It enables us to directly experience life without being clouded or distracted by memories, thoughts, fantasies or emotions.

Begin with a simple exercise. Each time you enter a room, do it with your left foot first. You may find yourself at first still unconsciously stumbling into the room. Patient practice will soon teach you to "know what you are doing." This exercise is simple but very effective. You will learn that you have no other choice but to make the effort to be mindful and be fully aware from one moment to the next. A failure to pursue this gives rise to the risk of sliding back into a profound state of unconsciousness.

Let us take a few steps together. You may say while doing so: "I can't help but wander along this path." You are right! It is the path of Beingness, here and now.

It suffices to simply move along the path, and, while doing such, to become increasingly alert, aware and mindful. One day you will realize that you do not really need all the pain and practice. You will ultimately realize that you have always been the ultimate truth, and will always be such.

Now take the first steps. What else are we to do? Do you already feel that you are completely in the place you have always wanted to reach? Do you realize that "It" is deep inside of you?

What exactly is this "It"? Do you want the answer right now?

We seek to find out what or who is posing the question. This "It" is what we want to find.

Sit down by the wayside and linger here on the path until you realize that you really do not have to go anywhere. The moment in which you realize this is the moment that you have grasped that you are already treading the pathless path. You already embody the entire distance on the path which you have already traversed. You are in the here and now when you put all your ideas and concepts aside.

The wonderful thing is that the path has always been here. The opportunity to "be on the path" has always been open to you. It transcends time and space and is thus the right thing for you at this very moment.

You become aware of the diamond concealed within you. The view was obscured by the sieve or filter of your ego and imagination. Your filter made you sick. This infliction stemmed from the accumulation of the "dirt" engendered by the hurts, anger, resentments and "negative" feelings in you.

Perceiving the diamond and rediscovering the divine spark

in you go hand in hand with releasing the ideas, opinions, concepts and fallacies stuck in your mind.

You are awakened to Being here and now, thanks to the grace of getting rid of all pre-conceived notions and ideas.

"Offer up your life to get it back."[19] This may be difficult for you to understand or act upon. What it actually means is letting go of concepts and ideas. You "let life be" as it really is. You are to dispense with all the baggage you accepted and internalized, and which you believed to be necessary.

You are free and cleansed once your inner sieve or smokescreen dissolves into nothingness. You need to become as transparent as glass in order not to be reflected in the mirror. You will learn to realize that you yourself are the glass letting light pass through.

When this glass is transparent, you will no longer be capable of being insulted, upset and hurt, because there will be nothing left to catch or absorb dirt or take things "personally."

Similarly, you will not be bloated with pride when you "achieve" something, or overjoyed if something happens which you think is good. You will no longer be riding the rollercoaster of life's ups and downs.

The feeling of relief is like being born again. It will cause you to laugh at your past life, in which you were always imprisoned in the illusions and delusions of your self-imposed mirror. Experiencing your Self is the most "disappointing" thing (for your ego) and yet, at the same time, the most beneficial way to get rid of your self-deceit and self-delusion. Leaving your (so-called) ego behind enables you to be whole and "holy."

You come to perceive the nonsense in your life. You sit down by the wayside. You are no longer a person being madly driven, one compelled to constantly experiment with new meditation techniques or spiritual paths. Of course, you are welcome on your path to Self-discovery to attend a meditation retreat or give in to the urge to spend time in a monastery. For many, the spiritual search only seems worthy if it involves trials and tribulations, if it becomes a full-time job absorbing all of your energy. The fact is that you are already blessed, that you have already been given the grace of being one with the Divine. You ARE everything, and there is nothing more!

If your soul does not realize it is already liberated, then everything you do is in vain.

Let us illustrate this with a parable. Imagine it was your task to show a person what defines you and your value as a human being. Would you fill your hands with pebbles and expect recognition? You would certainly choose to do so if you had nothing of greater value to offer. But you wouldn't choose pebbles if you actually possessed a priceless diamond! You would show your diamond.
Your Being is such a diamond.
Once you have thrown away your pebbles and leave them behind, you will be reborn, transparent and whole. You will be without the attachments, ties and everything else that you previously believed yourself to be. People often believe themselves to be worms constrained by misfortune, enchained by everything and everyone, unworthy creatures hopelessly, completely and utterly at the mercy of life.
Your new view of things will show you that this "It"—the Tao, God, the Divine, the Oneness, the Absolute, the Buddha Nature, the One Source—is boundless. The diamond which you ARE shines brightly. "It" is so hard that there is nothing that can scratch, damage or destroy it. It is sometimes called the "eternal

light" because it shines forever. You no longer need to fear losing your eternal life, because this "It"—which you are and which is in you—is without a beginning or end. "It" is limitless, boundless and infinite.

> "There is no place which is not imbued with the Way. It pervades all things and all sentient beings."
>
> —Ta-Mo

DO NOT BE AFRAID

Everything which is mortal in us remains on Earth. Why should we be afraid of losing the body we occupy? We know we have to leave it here. This assurance takes away any uncertainty we may have, and can free us from fear. Get used to this thought early on, and accept the death of your mortal self.

It could happen that you may physically die and be "disembodied" quite soon. But only that which is born can die.

We are actually the unborn—pure, eternal Being.

The Source, Tao, Buddha Nature, where the One goes back to, is above and beyond life and death.

This perspective is comforting. It means that we no longer have to worry about getting our share of eternity. Some religions have tried to make eternal life dependent on the way we live, on our convictions or deeds, or on our having the "right" faith. These religions claim that a certain way of living is necessary for persons to "earn" eternal life.

If this were the case, then eternity would be limited and finite, and would only be eternal for those who followed some specific concepts. Absolute Being is eternal, absolute, infinite, and completely unconditional. It has neither a beginning nor an end. It neither knows nor is dependent upon time, space or preconditions. The way in which Absolute Being manifests itself is not dependent on any forms.

We should also take a closer look at another fallacy. What kind of eternity has no end but supposedly has a beginning—that of birth? In this regard, all theologians have credibility problems. What kind of eternity seemingly begins at birth but does not end with death (at least for those who are "good")?

So let us mull this over. Let us return eternity to its rightful status, which of course nobody could ever have taken away from us. It was only used to threaten us and keep us in constant fear and trepidation. We were afraid that the laws applying to eternity would no longer apply in our case if our transgressions were overly grave.

This is nonsense.

If you are holding this fruit from the tree of your new understanding in your hand, then enjoy the taste of it. You are now capable of leaving behind you all that is fleeting, transient and mortal and of recognizing the eternal; that is, its endless and limitless nature. You are now capable of dispensing with fear.

To put things in a nutshell: accept the awareness that there is no end to eternity. That there is neither time nor space, and that there is neither a beginning nor an end, neither at birth nor at death. You ARE the Buddha Nature, unconditional and Absolute.

Your realization of this will put an end to all the pessimism about eternal damnation and all the worries about eternal life. "Rejoice—be not afraid!" These two recurring proclamations of Jesus, a compassionate Son of Man, comprise an attempt to make us instantaneously see things clearly.

There is no need to dwell upon the apparent motivation of the Pharisees and fundamentalists throughout the ages for their expert sowing of fear and anxiety. Things have changed nowadays. The number of people who are no longer prepared to be misled by these dire tidings is large and growing, as is those who are willing to deviate from the teachings of established religions.

The day may come in which the bulk of the followers of fear-based religions (some of which reneged long ago on their commitment to serve our inner Being) will find the courage to profess and stand up for their inner faith. The web of lies in which these religious leaders have gotten themselves entangled has become too extensive. It makes it questionable as to whether these religions will ever return to the original pathless paths that their founders revealed to us.

A new form of mysticism can no longer be suppressed. This is because the number of people who have listened to their inner call to seek and trod new paths—arising from their gifts of discernment and from their applications of meditation techniques—has reached a critical mass. Such people are prepared to delve deeper, to experiment and to use their experiences as the basis for their views. Such activities have always constituted the original foundation of mystical paths.

The realization that it is necessary to assume SELF-responsibility makes it easy to reflect and turn within while on the path.

As experience has shown, each year brings scientific findings contradicting the previous ones. Each year brings new instruments, processes and theories capable of better explaining the universe—and refuting past ones. This is a never-ending process. It implies that science will never be able to convincingly claim that it has found the absolute truth.

Has science ever been or will it ever be in a position to give us answers to all our questions?

Should the mystery of life ever be resolved, what would there still be left for us to do? Fortunately, the pathless path shows us how to deal with this.

Life is a mystery and enigma. We should accept the fact that there are no logical solutions to mysteries.

We ourselves are responsible for how we deal with this fact. If this were not the case, life would not be a miracle. We would not want to rob ourselves of the last remaining miracle. There is actually no danger of this happening. We simply do not have the capability of employing logic to solve every mystery.

Let us return to our path. We are now bearing responsibility for an indefinable mystery. Does this mean we have somewhere to return to? Or are we still here? In fact, we are still here. Where else should we be? There is always the here and now. There is no future life right now, and right now there is no past. There is only this very moment, and any worries we might have that this moment will pass by are unfounded! This moment is followed by the next moment. Each moment takes us to the next one in the here-now. So don't worry.

The only way to achieve calm and to be relaxed is by letting go of both the past and the future. The past only exists in your thoughts. You constantly suffer from the burdensome need to drag around your huge backpack, which is stuffed with memories and feelings about the past. We are calling upon you to consciously put down your heavy backpack for once and for all. This is the only way to get a feeling of relief.

Here is a good spot for setting it down. Don't worry; you can retrieve your backpack any time you need it. You may return to the past for brief interludes. However, once you have realized that we are always in the now, you will never "need" the contents of the backpack again. There is always a new moment, and this moment is eternal because it keeps on returning.

The future is also only in our minds. All the expectations, hopes, fears and misgivings for and about it clutter up and distort your future. It is in any case often quite different than your expectations for it. Heed the (proverbial) Eleventh Commandment: "Do not let yourself be deceived." When you realize that the future does not yet exist in the here and now, you will be able to dispense with the need to conduct the thought processes cluttering up your mind.

You might argue that "a sensible person needs to consider the future and what it may bring." You are right. We have to make plans for the future. Please allow us to point out that we never said that the future does not exist in the future. Live in the moment, in the here-now, and you will put the future in its rightful place, and live it in the right way.

The apprehensions and fears that we harbor about the future are often more frightening than what we actually experience. Turn your mind to a moment in which you were confronted with a danger and in which you ended up doing the right thing. Did you feel the same level of anxiety and trepidation in handling this peril as you had when worrying about this threat beforehand?

You know exactly what we mean. This is because you have frequently had such experiences. It might be embarrassing to admit that when the future you had so feared finally came to pass, it wasn't always as dire as you had imagined. The inevitable confrontation with the future that you so had wanted to avoid often gives rise to new opportunities. Every crisis opens up a window of opportunity. Such crises often turn out to be less grim than we had expected.

Casting aside the backpack of the past enables you to let go of your fears and anxieties for the future. Do not fear! You will achieve happiness by emptying your mind of all such contents. This will give your mind a purity and clarity of being.

We would not seem to have progressed very far down the pathless path. Are you impatient with us? No reason to be. We never said the path was long. Should you have thought so, you probably expected something very challenging. People mistakenly believe that one has to struggle mightily to achieve insights, to act in a superhero-like manner. You thought that we would walk with difficulty, strive to achieve something indescribable, or at least discuss a lot of things. Do you sense your inner desire to make things more complicated?

Do you understand what we mean? You do not have to "carry the world on your shoulders."

Moving along the pathless path does not entail the egocentric urge to do something extraordinarily great. In contrast, it is about letting go of doing. There is something wonderful about simply sitting down, and, by doing nothing else except for sitting, being right in the here-now. You are already here. You do not have to plan to undertake any more changes in yourself. Nor do you have to leave this room. Already being here means you do not require any more time to get "there." The pathless path is the inner counterpart to such a physical pilgrimage as the famous Way of St. James to Santiago de Compostela in Spain.

Enlightenment, or whatever you call it, is above and beyond time and space.

"It"—Tao, God, the Divine, the Oneness, the Absolute, the Buddha Nature, the One Source, the Self—is already here. Our "blindness" prevents us from perceiving or experiencing it right away. This 'It' is concealed to us by being buried under a whole lot of garbage. Trying to see it is akin to trying to see your reflection in a mirror covered with dust. In actual fact, we are incapable of finding a mirror. This is because there really was no mirror in the first place[20]. In light of this, "where is the dust to settle?"

This question is a koan from Hui Neng[21]. Its ultimate impact is to dissolve everything. It does not leave you with anything, nor is there any place you could even leave a trace of anything behind.

THE EGO

"And blindness keeps us entrapped." I, Genro, penned this. It forms part of a lyrical text accompanying a photo of my son. Both text and photo were in an earlier book of mine. At the time of formulation, the sentences seemed to be writing themselves on the paper. I now read the book with astonishment. It must have been the case that I was a tool for these words and still am. Although I was imprisoned at the time in the ego, I was still capable of letting it happen.

In this book, another kind of surrendering to Existence and trust in the One Presence prevails and serves as the basis for it. Once more, something is writing itself in and through us. Today everything is One, because there is nobody here who feels he is separate or isolated. I AM the doer, the doing and the deed.

Where do you end, and where does the next person begin?

Why do you feel separate? Do you think you are someone special?

It turns out that we enjoy making distinctions and seeing differences. Our decision-making ability usually ends up distinguishing between no and yes, Yin and Yang, good and evil, right and wrong. In fact, this ability creates seeming opposites. In reality, these are complements of each other.

This ability causes us to think ourselves separate, and not or no longer whole or "holy." We cast doubt upon ourselves and our existence. We are full of misgivings. The ego differentiates, distinguishes and divides in order to create disparity, and is proud of being seemingly different. The ego protects itself through separation, defines itself on the basis of distinction, and builds protective walls around itself. The ego is pure resistance. It casts a glow of radiance or retreats into a shell of its own making, where it dwells in dark confines.

This fearful shutting up inside ourselves creates the confinement that prevents our life energy—also referred to as our vital energy or Chi—from flowing freely. Let go, let it be, let yourself be! Allow life and the Divine to live in and through you. Allow It to live in you!

You separate yourself from the wholeness of Existence, the Oneness, whenever you believe yourself to be someone special and unique, someone who has a certain function, role or position. You separate yourself from the Oneness whenever you believe you are someone with certain tasks to perform, with a very specific personal touch, with special characteristics and with individual talents. These beliefs make you the epitome of resistance instead of being whole and allowing the Self to live in you.

One option for you is to sit down for just a moment on this stone lying along the wayside, and for you to accept everything you consider to be confining and restricting. You could continue seeing yourself as the perceiving person, one who considers Existence to be separate from him. This insistence makes you the one with the (mis)belief in duality, in separateness. But there is yet another option. This is to give up believing that you are only a part of it. Upon doing such, you will partake of the whole. How glorious this is!

The realization that "you have to lose your life to find it" ("For whoever who will save his life shall first have to lose it"[22]) has proven to be true in manifold and ever-changing ways. In the Buddha's words, "In Heaven and on Earth, I alone am the honored one." (The "I" is the I AM, not the individual self or the Buddha as a historical person.)

Whoever surrenders to life will live it more fully. Giving up your ego means getting a real life, one in which we are neither alone nor lonely, but All-One, all-embracing. When you have become All-One, you will also be able to state that you are the only enlightened one, as Buddha put it. The fact of the matter is that there is only One. There is nothing outside of you because you have realized yourself, and realize your-self in the Self.

Goethe also made this point. He stated that people have to undergo a form of spiritual death (before they physically die) prior to their achieving "enlightenment". This death entails a relinquishment of the ego, of attachment to forms, and of the concept of duality. As Goethe went on to say, doing this will put you on the path towards awakening to your inherent nature and towards becoming what you truly are. "And so long as you haven't experienced this: to die and so to grow, you are only a troubled guest on the dark earth."[23]

One is not capable of putting a name to that upon which not even dust can settle. Nor can one precisely describe it. It is the all-reflecting and all-encompassing consciousness that underlies all Existence and all that Is. You cannot denote something that comprises time and space, form and emptiness. You cannot denote something that encompasses to "die and become," "to be or not to be"; something that is "without a beginning or end." There is Nobody who can perceive and realize this. Real life exists upon there being no more ego and no more egoistical processes focusing on the individual "I."

Only the Divine laughs when unity, the One, arises from duality.

We are not capable of making this decision on our own. Requisite to do such is grace. ("Not my will, but Thy will be done."[24]) We can only act when we do such without intent. How can the holder-on become the one letting go? The ego can only disappear once it is completely undone and once it has been absorbed in the struggle. Grace opens up a way to enter the Kingdom of Heaven, in which there is a complete lack of all wanting and of deliberate action.

For grace, it does not matter if, when, where and how it takes place.

How long do you have to sit here until you understand? You are free to wander on should you not be gaining any insights. You will finally have a chance again when all efforts become too strenuous and wandering becomes too painstaking and exhausting.

Allow us to continue talking to you while we are moving on the path. Should our talk not adequately entertain you, look for another companion or wander untiringly by yourself. If you do not understand us, it will be cumbersome and arduous for you to continue seeking here. This may sound arrogant. We don't attach much importance to being understood. The story we are telling interacts directly with your ego. This may cause the listener to feel hurt.

The ego is capable of tremendously inflating itself. It gets bloated from being satiated. This condition causes it to suffer just as much as when it feels empty and hollow. Our longing resonates in our egos; we want to be liberated from suffering and to allow the divine spark to shine a light. This one glowing spirit and light shine brightly and clearly in you. We refer to this when we say the Sanskrit word "Namaste"[25,] when greeting others.

I, Genro, remember a student of mine. I greeted her by saying "Namaste." She asked me if every single person possesses this light. I replied: "Every sentient being, every person, animal, plant and stone, in fact all of Existence is permeated with this."

Her answer was: "If everyone is infused with this light, this path is not interesting to me. I want to have something that belongs only to me."

Her statement reflects the work of the ego. We would deny ourselves the right to enjoy "eternal life" due to our desire to stand out and be an island onto ourselves. Egocentrically bloated, a person focuses on what "belongs" to him. On the basis of his own tiny self, his strength and consciousness, he separates himself from others by wanting to "have." Yet a person also does not want to be lonely. He can celebrate his supposed victory and complain about his loneliness right afterwards. How paradoxical!

What we are discussing in this chapter is the overriding and arrogant self-image which we have come to assume and accept, which we have deluded ourselves into thinking is the truth, and which distorts everything. It overshadows us, keeps us imprisoned, mercilessly ties us up, and keeps us enchained.

Kings in Europe used to have court jesters. By the same token, there is a story about an emperor of China who had a Chan Master. The propensity of Chan Masters to tell the truth often led to their falling from grace. One day, the Chan Master reproached the emperor. The Master told him that his ego had expanded to attain gigantic proportions, and told the emperor to relinquish his hold on it. Such "blow-ups" are common in leaders. The emperor's response was to say: "Master, show me my ego! How can I let go of it when I cannot even recognize it?"

The Master's response put his cleverness and toughness on display. Such Masters are the embodiment of the truth. They act with firmness towards everybody, including emperors. The Masters do not make any distinctions between emperors and other sentient beings. The Masters are well aware that the true Self, the real person exists above and beyond, and is independent of an individual's social status, reputation, position, income and possessions.

The Chan Master's response was to lay an effective trap whose bait was disrespect. He said to the emperor: "Your Majesty, your question was so stupid that I felt it unworthy of being answered!" In response, the emperor turned red with rage. He called for his henchmen, and came within a hair of beheading his own Zen Master.

The reason why this beheading didn't place was the Chan Master's response just in the nick of time (had he failed to do so, this story would have never come into being): "Majesty, why do you want to behead me? All I was trying to do was to show you your ego. All I did was to give you the answer to your question! The ego is what arose inside of you, what caused your rage and wrath and what is making you feel so much hate for your teacher. Your ego is what clouds your senses, dulls your perception and limits your consciousness!" In response, showing that he had completely understood his master, the emperor made a deep bow to him.

You can well appreciate the extent to which this insight pertains to us! We have the capability to learn how to transcend the ego, should someone both explain the theory behind doing such, and should she or he lead us in the above manner to enlightenment. We can transcend it if we learn to observe how the ego grows and expands and if we perceive how it takes possession of us, rendering us completely unaware and unknowing in the process.

Your true Being exists. The real you is here! The ego is simply functionality, imagination and fantasy, and you will be instantly liberated from it upon being mindful and observing it! You are not separate or isolated. You do not have to put up walls, nor do you need to wildly throw punches all around you. Instead, "let His will be done."

We realize that we do not gain anything by pursuing separation and isolation or by trying to "stand out" and "distinguish" ourselves from others. Detachment from others and from the One may give you a supposedly distinct personality, but in this case you are only part of the One. If you allow yourself to be Nobody, everything belongs to you and is in you, and you are in everything at that moment. There is nothing outside of you! There is also Nobody left who can be separate, for example, from the One Source of all Being.

In other words, there is Nobody who is wandering along the pathless path. You can also say "two nobodies—you and the wanderer." But there is no such thing as two nobodies. Let us simply say that Nobody is on the pathless path. Somebody can sit down somewhere, but Nobody can never sit anywhere, because Nobody can sit nowhere.

If the path arises from wandering, and Nobody wanders on the pathless path—a way which is without a path—then there is actually no path at all. That is why it is termed "pathless."

There is Nobody wandering along the path. There is only wandering.

Let us continue on the path. We hope you perceive that it is comprised of serenity, calmness and letting go.

It's wonderful! Feel this deep, pervasive, divine tranquility. Everything is calm and tranquil all around us, and there is no noise. There is Nobody to be disturbed and Nobody who disturbs. No one "has" enlightenment. Nobody can grasp or "receive" enlightenment. Enlightenment is you. "If Nobody is there, then I will reveal the truth to you." This is an old koan from Zen Buddhism. It is a puzzle that can help you to open yourself to the "Holy Spirit," should that be the way things should be.

There is a story about one pupil who hopes to get the answer he needs when nobody else is around. When he and the Master are alone late one evening, he asks the Master what truth is. The Master affectionately takes his pupil's arm and leads him to the next bamboo grove. Then he points to a small plant and says, "This bamboo is short" and subsequently points to a larger one and says, "This bamboo is long." The Master's failure to get a response from the student is due to the latter's still being Somebody—identifying with his ego.

The explanation of the Master is thus based on bamboo branches of varying lengths. It provides another clear indication of what he is trying to convey. The small bamboo has not yet reached the size and length (and thus the degree of Self-realization) of the larger one. What the Master meant to state is: "When your ego has been transcended and when there is Nobody left, then you will naturally know the '"Isness" to be the truth."

Any acceptance of "Suchness" is simultaneously an acceptance of "non-acceptance," (because there is no ego left to accept), of "not being able to find" or the acceptance of the never-ending desire to search. Isn't such a discovery enlightening?

People who think it is necessary to make enormous efforts to increase their level of Self-awareness will grow dispirited upon discovering their inability to cast light upon their illuminated selves—which they already are. Their Self always shines brightly—regardless of what they strive to do. In reality, every individual who wrongly believes that he has to carry the world on his shoulders has to learn to accept not to do this any longer.

Your restlessness, your wish to set forth your search may return. You are also able to accept it—as if you had a choice in the first place! At this moment, the blessing so long desired is that of a deep feeling of inner peace. Use "in-sight" to eliminate intellectual stubbornness. Upon doing that, we will be able to accept, embody and be our "Isness."

Being human beings is comprised of how the Isness breathes us, lives us, beats our hearts. Egoism in all its facets and functions, whether burdensome or uplifting, is also deeply human.

If this is the case, how is this to be dealt with? The answer: by employing "kung-ans," as they are known in China, or "koans" as they are called elsewhere. Each of these is an enigma that cannot be solved through the employment of intellect. Koans are stories expressing the mysteries of life. They are tools designed to help penetrate our cognitive armor. Dealing with hopelessly unsolvable and seemingly unanswerable questions can serve as an alarm clock helping us to wake up to the present moment. Koans are a traditional tool that is still used in the Rinai school of the Chan masters to help liberate people's minds.

A few examples: "How do you take the first step from the top of a sixty-foot flagpole?" "Does a dog have the Buddha Nature?" And how about this one: "Show me the sound of one hand (clapping)."

In actual fact, many of us already have our own "life koans" to deal with, even though we may not be aware of their existence. They may well be the most difficult ones to solve, as difficult as cracking a hard nut. This is because they consist of personal challenges to be mastered, past experiences to be dealt with, problems to be solved, and obstacles to be overcome before we get to experience inner peace and serenity, and to move ahead on the path.

If you go to a monastery to study Zen and you do not have the answer to a koan posed to you, you may receive thirty blows with a stick. And even if you do have an answer, you may also be hit thirty times! What alternatives do you have? This is one of the ways in which Chan and Zen masters exert a healing effect on their students (without actually physically hurting them). What appears to be a brutal act is actually an expression of their compassionate willingness to help.

These blows are administered using the "Kyoasaku," or the "awakening stick." The monk on duty uses the stick to keep you awake. Its prodding stimulates your shoulder muscles. When done at the proper acupuncture points, this prodding can stimulate a person's circulation and prevent sleepiness. Some people in monasteries and retreats spend up to eight hours a day sitting in intensive meditation. Most of this time is spent sitting on the floor. Some beginners experience terrible pain in their legs. At such sessions, the only thing briefly interrupting this meditation is "Kinhin," which is slow, meditative walking. Pain also has the capability to keep you awake, alert and conscious, in the same manner as the receiving of a blow administered by the awakening stick.

But there is more to such blows. Receiving them gives you the opportunity to realize the truth and to awaken to the alertness characterizing enlightenment. This is in contrast to the deep sleep of blindness.

Zen has a story to offer about this. A student requests: "Master, show me the ultimate truth." And the Master's response is to hit him with the awakening stick! It is the only thing he can do in this situation. The bottom line is that there may be no other viable alternative at his disposal at that moment. He wants to compassionately try to shake up the seeker, who is imprisoned in a state of deep sleep, so as to enable him to enter a state of awareness. The brief pain felt by the pupil is a wake-up call. We do not know whether or not the pupil will experience the grace of enlightenment. Despite this, the fact that the experience of enlightenment does not take place in our concept of time and space is irrelevant here.

Are you capable of realizing your true Self and Beingness to begin with, and at this very moment, as we move gently down it with you for your benefit? How we would also like to be able to awaken you with a well-aimed blow!

You can see that there is no way out! So you will have to come up with something else. Let grace work in you and come upon you. Be ready.

Why strive for enlightenment? For what purpose? Instead of getting entangled in mind games, simply do all the right things at just the right time without any defined purpose whatsoever, for no reason at all, or let them happen. Don't get caught up and entangled any more. Sit on the shore of life, and watch things as they pass by.

Observe, be a witness and be free, without attachments.

Many people revel, even wallow, in their existential dilemma. Such people are convinced that it is the destiny of human beings. As they are incapable of being observers, they identify with their human predicament. They accept it as being normal, even though our "normal" state is Oneness. However, the worse the consequences of egoistic processes are, and the more suffering and pain there is, the more people have the chance to grow and mature. The existential question is: "Who are you—the seeker?"

The disorientation which overcomes us from time to time

causes us to cast doubt on the underlying sense and purpose of life. Doubting, one of our favorite pastimes, is the inevitable consequence of dualism. Separating, dividing and distinguishing are fatal, as Goethe expresses it so well.

How does it come about that we lose sight of the unity of all Existence after we are born? How do we end up by falling into a state of duality, the two-ness of good and evil? According to Traditional Chinese Medicine (TCM), duality is the reason why we are burdened with kidney ailments. Therapy might relieve the suffering arising from this disharmony but cannot heal the underlying cause.

You are intact, whole and healed once you no longer believe you are lost.

Wholeness is realizing that you are undivided, the eternal One. Then you are no longer afraid of having to find your-Self when pursuing your lifelong search.

However, until this happens, most people try to distract themselves from their primordial state by lingering on the periphery of Existence, which is where the wheel of time revolves. In this state, distractions are considered to be essential, and substitute gratifications assume the task of keeping us alive. While wandering in the darkness through deep valleys, we collect and accumulate so-called "treasures" (such as possessions, knowledge and status), and even take pride in this! We vigorously defend what we have accumulated so greedily, are jealous and envious of others, experience hate, and have doubts about the One being unfathomable.

Salvation takes place once we accept that the Oneness is unfathomable and mysterious. The Oneness embodies both our salvation and that which is irresolvable.

We place our trust in our egos instead of realizing ourselves to be part of and One with Existence and, as such, both infinite and eternal. The ego is the most human of all dysfunctions. And to make things worse, we are even proud of all these attachments, identifications and negative emotions. Clever lobbies have always made use of this to exploit and thus manipulate people.

Our bodies manifest and store these misbegotten passions and memories. TCM describes the ailments arising from the reliance on the ego in such picturesque terms as "sticky mucus," "toxic heat" and "harmful wind." This figurative language enables us to easily see how our behavior damages our inner organs, causing us to suffer immensely in the process, both physically and psychologically.

People who carry their pasts with them as ongoing traumas frequently exhibit liver problems. According to TCM, the liver is the organ which stores our past memories and experiences. In contrast, people who harbor fears and apprehensions of the future harm their lungs, and are thus scarred both physically and psychologically.

Therapy offers approaches capable of discerning the reasons for people's behavior. To do such, therapy looks at these from an intellectual or emotional perspective. Notwithstanding this, therapy is not capable of providing the ultimate solution. It provides help and relief for a foreseeable period of time, but usually does not assuage a person's fundamental lack of orientation.

It is meditation that has the ability to get you to look inside yourself. This gives rise to such blessings as fearlessness, bliss and the chance to enjoy the grace of the infinite, eternal Being. Poets, mystics and sages have given us an enticing inkling of what lies ahead when we meditate. However, these mere words cannot do full justice to something that is ultimately indescribable.

Although therapy can have a beneficial, soothing and alleviating effect, it generally does not penetrate to the heart of the matter. By way of contrast, meditation enables a person to venture into the center of her or his being, dispelling the evil afflicting us in the process. It does so in a manner which is new to our understanding.

This step represents our having come full circle on the spiritual path. Reconnecting with your inner being is taking the individual, selfless path of love and compassion, with the realization and unconditional acceptance of what is and whatever happens.

Founders of religions have tried to demonstrate their having delineated the right path. While doing this, they have ventured the claim that truth can only be realized in and through them. This is because they have lived and practiced it. Nowadays, we are not always in a position to understand exactly what they originally meant. The consequence of this is the plethora of misinterpretations.

There are cases of people who were enlightened and who had a depth of faith and of spiritual understanding equal to that of the founders of religions, but were slandered and even killed by religious institutions. This was the fate which befell Jesus. Think about how the great mystics Jakob Böhme and Meister Eckhart were treated. Or consider the roles played by inquisitions and religious wars in the long and sad story of humanity. These cases are analogous to what has transpired in the world of politics. By way of example: the way Athens treated Socrates. The inevitability of his fate stemmed from the inability of the ego of the masses to accept the truth. They were and are willing to fight to the bitter end to suppress it.

Please now consider the major works of wise individuals. As is the case with flowers in the desert, these works cast a gentle glimmer of hope—based on love and compassion—into the vast wastelands formed by dry, theological texts and their sober, bloodless arguments. Why do people seem to be so afraid of these works?

In any case, misconceived teachings end up leading nowhere or to absurdities. We have absolutely no need for legal regulations that dictate which religious paths we are to follow or reject. We are citizens of countries in which rule of law is said to prevail. As such, we have the right to enjoy our privacy. Privacy excludes the interference of the state in our personal sphere. This enables us to do whatever we view as being essential for our inner Being, provided that such does not harm anyone else.

As Posa said to King Philip of Spain, "Let the people have freedom of thought."[26] Should we have or demand less from our rulers today? Freedom of religion forms part of declarations of human rights. We should not allow any government, institution or other spiritual path, including major world religions, to tell us how to pursue our spirituality.

People are prone to criticizing others. This especially applies to moral issues. We were educated to believe that we are required to follow the vast body of rules, precepts and commandments imposed upon us in order to be "worthy." However, the Kingdom of God is within us. Does this not mean that we are whole, complete, eternal, Absolute and unconditional from the very start? If this is the case, nothing can be added or taken away from our inherent nature.

The more mindful you are, the more you will be able to clearly discern the real motivation behind the texts and deeds of people aiming to mislead and entrap us. We should—for once and for all—say "goodbye and good riddance" to such people.

The important thing is to mindfully observe how they are and how they act. In many cases, they no longer share the motives or love of a Moses, Jesus, Krishna, Zarathustra, Mohammed or Buddha.

A further problem is our worship of such other false gods as consumer products. This worship has caused stores to become modern-day temples of consumption. Our modern-day gurus take the guises of talk show hosts consumed by TV ratings; offices churn out the offerings of mass media; the creators of Facebook, Twitter, virtual reality and the like—not to mention the latest "Internet stars." These people are rarely aware of their responsibility towards others. Consumers often unconditionally believe what is being displayed on their TV screens, computers or electronic devices.

Whatever comes is bound to disappear and to have no lasting effect. That is the nature of the relative, material world in which we live.

The latest trends, fads or whatever is "in" are only temporary and illusive in nature. In contrast, infinite, Absolute Being is eternal, is not subject to limitations and restrictions, and is above and beyond space and time. It is cause and effect but is completely independent of it all. We are all independent and unconditional!

NOTHING IS EVERYTHING

WHAT YOU CAN achieve is a quiet and mindful observation of the world. It is now or never! Engaging in observation may seem to be very complicated, difficult and boring in the relative, material world. However, it has always been a simple thing in the realm of the Infinite. The ego experiences this process to be so cumbersome and burdensome that it calls attention to itself when acting as a high-performance Something. Another favorite recourse of the ego is to show that it is the tormented and agonized I. However, what really exists is in a state of the eternal, everlasting Now. Nothing is on the outside. Nor is it an exception or above and beyond it.

Nevertheless, knowing this does not prevent us from moving on. This is because we do not care to remain seated, be it in school or here on the path. But, by resting in observation, you will immediately realize how wonderful it is to listen to the birds, to feel the warm sun on your skin and the freshness and coolness of the air when you breathe, and to smell the variety of scents in the forests and meadows. We will bow down to you when you succeed in overcoming the thoughts and inner dialogues taking place in your mind—and your mind's incessant philosophizing, speculating and brooding as well.

You will come to realize that this calmness, tranquility

and serenity—along with a profound peace and serenity—are present, and have always been so, even though we were afraid we had lost it all or never possessed these things in the first place.

They are all still here! All the values and small things which make us happy are still here. In the East, Buddha says, "Sat, Chit and Ananda," which means Being, Conscious Being and Bliss. All of them are one and inseparable. There is nothing else! Is this inconceivable to you?

We frequently have the opposite impression, namely that we are often unaware and unhappy, that life is full of ups and downs, and that it consists of "having and wanting." You know by now that there is something in us (yes, the ego) which makes it seem that this is the case. If the Divine no longer seems to be worth striving for, then this something robs us of divine grace, our Being, Conscious Being and Bliss. Accordingly, we dwell in a state of being unaware. It is our present-day reality, and is thus completely normal to us. Existence accepts this. Who are you to quarrel with all of Existence?

Moods and behavioral patterns—the functions of the ego—come and go, and have no basis or reality in the Eternal. Your ego is NOT you!

Do you realize the price you are paying by being ego-centered? You are whole and intact when you accept that the ego does not belong to you, when you realize yourself to be the non-ego.

Only grace enables you to be in a state of emptiness!

We can only perceive what is physical and discernible with our senses. But as the Buddhists say, "Form is emptiness and emptiness is form."[27] It is not a question of nothingness. There is no duality but rather interdependence and Oneness. One cannot exist without the other. Why is the clay pot so valuable? Its usefulness stems from the space that it creates. This emptiness can be used to store liquid. The house has value because of its walls, and the space created among them. What would the stars be without the backdrop of the rest of the universe?

You are the all-encompassing Self where the supposed "you" no longer dominates.

Rejoice at the emptiness in you, in which there is no longer a sieve or filter to capture garbage. There is no place in you to deposit anything. If Nobody is there, the Divine can enter! Then this emptiness is all-encompassing, boundless and infinite, and nothing is on the outside any longer.

Not even an ant can creep around outside of your consciousness![28]

Let us live with our hearts wide open to feeling, experiencing and accepting Existence with all our senses. This is true liberation! This comes when we do exercises designed to help us breathe more freely and to be deeply relaxed, and when we open our chests like window sashes or barn doors. This comes when we use our imagination to set aside our imaginary shoulder girdles and the related burdens, enabling us to relax. It is as if, in a single dramatic move, one suddenly allowed the birds to fly freely and be free of everything in them which had been kept locked up. In breathing out, we let go and set free all the hurts, scars, injuries that we have ever experienced or felt, that we think we are responsible for.

All these burdens detach themselves from our hearts and are released from our chests when we let go of our burdens, when we meditate, and when we accept Existence as it is. Such a process cleanses us and sets us free. It makes us empty, teaches us not to hold back anything, and show us how to be as porous and permeable as a canal without barriers. Nothing can stick to or attach itself to the pure walls of our Being. Transparency results in invulnerability, in just the same way that glass allows light to pass through. Once this happens, we do not mean that you should be cold, uncaring, indifferent, unfeeling or insensitive towards others, as people sometimes falsely interpret this. We are referring to how you will perceive and realize yourself to be: as intact, healed and sacred.

This pure, sacred emptiness which feels very light is our original and primordial state.

We are talking about the particular state of Being that Zen defines to be the awareness of enlightened consciousness. It is defined by the word "Shikantaza," which means "only sitting." When this state is achieved, there is no more relying on meditation techniques, breathing exercises, mantras, rosary beads or contemplation, and no more activity. Instead of all that, we focus on simply sitting on the meditation cushion and surrendering to the force of gravity. To put it simply, we exist as pure Being.

Zen Masters say: "This is the original state. It existed before there was a father or mother." Jesus says, "Before Abraham was, I AM."[29] You can see the consensus here! If you have read Kabir, you can perhaps understand what he means when he talks about opening up space in yourself for Existence to enter.[30] When the ego gives way to the Self, there is room for the ocean, which can pour forth as the dewdrops of your Being.

Originally Kabir believed that a dewdrop dissolving into the ocean was the best way to describe the state of entering and embracing the all-encompassing Oneness. Later in his life, he apparently delved into the Oneness even more deeply. Shortly before Kabir's death, his son described his father's change in his perception of the experience of enlightenment. "It is not the dewdrop of individuality which dissipates into the ocean of the One Consciousness, but just the opposite! The entire ocean of Cosmic Consciousness flows into the dewdrop of self-realized Being."

It is indeed asking a lot of you to empty yourself and to create a seeming void, but the effort pays off! Can we do it? Can we experience the moment when the ego gives up, when it finally accepts that there is nothing to "do"? Emptiness, the void, already prevails when there is nothing to discover. One calls this "content-less" emptiness. It is actually freedom from your-self. Do we have to prove this now? You cannot prove it, even if you do as much research as you want.

Search for yourself, your ego, essence, Being or whatever you consider yourself to be or think you are. Start searching right away while we are wandering along the path.

No matter how long you search, you won't find anything. You cannot describe or grasp the Self, no matter how much you try. Do you now believe that it is completely empty? Enjoy the infinite space creating this experience in you. Let yourself be filled by Existence itself, and be fulfilled by the Isness, by everything that is. Emptiness allows the Divine to enter.

There is nothing, absolutely nothing except for the Self!

The Self cannot be compared to the limitations and restrictions that you place upon yourself and that you believe yourself to be a victim of. Nor can the Self be compared to the very minuscule part which you identify as constituting the "I." The Self is also not comparable to what you painstakingly tried to make out of your life, to what is supposedly unique and special in you, that something which you attempted to completely blow out of proportion. The Self is far removed from the ego with which you identified and which you hoped to enhance and glamorize.

If you are only part of the whole, you are only a paltry and measly attachment worried about the purpose and meaning of it all! Now you can be everything and realize that your inherent Being is the all-encompassing Oneness, not the egoistic, body-based creature you thought you were.

How do you feel when there is only wandering along the path, and neither a person who is wandering nor a path to tread upon? How do you feel when both subject and object have disappeared, and the only thing remaining is wandering? Let go and allow yourself to experience what is taking place in the here-now. This is the way it goes, as your heart keeps beating for you, as your breath breathes you, as life lives you.

You will be Being just like "Sat," you will be Conscious Being like "Chit," and Bliss just like "Ananda."

The fact is that Bliss is our original state of Being!

Our way of Beingness consists of simply wandering without a separate you and me. There is only movement. Unfortunately, you have to listen right now to all this yickety-yak from us. You can change the situation simply by chasing us away. However, keep us around if you are still not capable of being the all-encompassing Oneness, if you still think that there is still something you need to find, discover, explore or investigate. We hope that we will be more of a help to you than an obstacle in your way.

What exists all around us when we move? It is a singing, a

joyous celebration of the birds—It sings. It is a blossoming, a sprouting, a growing, an incredible fragrance—It blooms. It is a heat-giving radiance, a feeling on your skin—It feels. It lives.

It is a dance, and this dance lives in and through the dancer who has forgotten himself. There is only the dancing.

Everything which expresses itself in the dance is divine. It comprises the divine spark in all this vibrant Being.

Nothing dances outside of our Consciousness.

THE INDESCRIBABLE MYSTERY

One cannot wander along the pathless path because it is pathless. Is this an unsolvable dilemma? There is no path, but we have already agreed that we are moving. We could also use the examples of the doorless barrier and the iron flute[31], which are similar to all koans in Zen. It is obvious that you do not see the same sky when viewing it from a variety of windows. Nor do you perceive light in the same way when it is cast by different lamps.

If we each call upon our mind to create definitions that it is not able to produce because of its limited perspective, we will sooner or later realize that we have resorted to using the wrong instrument. Discursive thinking is unsuited to achieve and realize the ultimate truth. Notwithstanding this, we are forced to discuss things. This entails accepting the inherent reality of our intellects and minds. How else are we to do it?

Words, numbers and symbols comprise products of a mind which functions logically. Logic is limited by itself.

In other words, how is it possible for something that is inherently limited to grasp what is infinite and endless? It is important to point out that this infinity also encompasses the mind, but the mind will never be able to grasp and encompass the infinite truth. This is the first handicap that we face. It is also the reason why Masters try to shake up their pupils and thus raise their awareness by resorting to screaming, hitting or shocking them—without beating around the bush.

Here is the story about the Emperor of China, who called together all the prominent people in his kingdom to honor his Zen Master and to listen to his pearls of wisdom. After all the requisite preparations had been made, thousands of dignitaries from science, religion, politics and the arts traveled long distances and ultimately converged upon the hall to listen to Chan Master Huang-Po and his preaching. The Master took the high seat. The hall became completely quiet, and the unbelievably large crowd sat in reverent silence and waited to hear the Master's instructions. Huang-Po hit the floor with his stick and said, "As there is nothing else to mention, this meeting is over!"

How significant this statement is!

He took the opportunity to get people to realize the truth by provocatively shattering their views, expectations and idle speculation. It is hardly possible to be closer to the ultimate truth. There are few statements as meaningful and important as the one made by Huang-Po. Everything is contained in his all-encompassing speech. The Oneness cannot be expressed. It is here and now, and there is no time for us to lose.

When people listen to this story, you can see the incomprehension in their faces. Many of them cannot make heads or tails of such a splendid declaration about The Last Things.[32] Our ego considers the demeanor of Huang-Po to be destructive. The Master's behavior rubs us the wrong way, and the ego shrugs it off as trivial, ridiculous, contrived and even pointless.

We want answers to our questions. So we often get explanations. Many of them are from people who are actually not competent. These explanations confuse or deceive us, take us on detours, and temporarily rob us of the opportunity to gain Self-realization.

If someone tries to explain to you what "Tao" means, you should quickly turn your back on this person and take to your heels. Buddhists say: "Whoever uses the word Buddha should clean his mouth." Lao-Tzu says: "One cannot express the Tao in words."[33] It is similarly written that we are not to make images of God.[34]

However, all of the above has gone to our heads again. So let us return to the center of our Being and to our legs, which move us. There is only wandering.

When the Cosmic Existence is dancing, and when we are part of this dance, we should not allow ourselves to be earnest, unless there is a person on our path whose name is Earnest! Being earnest is a sickness on the path. It is an obstacle to our moving forward, works against us, and is a product of our ego. It gorges itself on the pus of the moralizing Moloch that continually feeds on itself and that wants to restrict people's freedom and personal space.[35] Accordingly, carefully ascertain whether or not people who claim that they embody the Oneness and live in freedom are free from being serious.

Let us enjoy the tranquility and sit down. Do nothing but sit! We have explained to you, after all, that it is probably a good idea to see what Is. If you succeed in getting a glance at the truth, there will be nothing else. You will burst out laughing with relief. Or rather, one should say: It will laugh at you. You will experience a wonderful, deeply heartfelt joy. When you let go, your body may sweat. You may also experience a feeling of well-being and bliss. It will be accompanied by total physical and mental relaxation.

Everything that has burdened you and that you have desperately held on to, all the tensions, worries and troubles that plagued you and inflicted incalculable suffering, will disappear, and you will be "saved." You and your ego-based life will no longer be in the way, and you will be free of your limited self. You may think it is dangerous to let go and lose control. But our challenge is to "die before we die"—to awaken to our original Being, which is unborn and undying.

But let us not engage in theorizing! That would be useless. It is there, in walking, dancing, singing; in the arts, in sports and in all of the activities in which you forget your-self. It has always been there.

It can be found in the present moment, much more so than in all the parables and examples provided by founders of religions and "life teachers." It is far more valuable than the wisdom contained in "holy" books, no matter how enlightening they seem to be.

Celebrate Existence. Let Existence celebrate you, as it continuously does anyway.

You can exist, simply be, and live just like a child. A childlike disposition means being playful, means experiencing life profoundly with innocent eyes, and means being open to what life offers. You do not have to "have" anything for this but only to let yourself be. Allow yourself to let go and be your-Self, to be serene and composed right here by the wayside.

Meditation, the means by which you can return to your inner center, shows you how to observe your breathing and thoughts. It is a vital process, as it calms your mind. You can even practice it above and beyond your periods of meditation, on a non-stop basis. By the way, meditation is not only the "sitting down" kind. You can meditate in every moment and thus make it part of your daily life! Everything that works is good!

NON-THINKING

Doesn't a river flow without seeking? Doesn't a bird sing beautifully without a specific intention? What is it exactly that we are looking for on this path?

One thing is certain, and that is uncertainty! You need courage to continue wandering without having intention, while knowing that you are in a state of not knowing. Is there really a guide and is someone really being guided?

The Self expresses itself in both the Master and the pupil! Is there a problem with this? Where are the explanations and advice necessary to help us understand?

Don't let yourself be misled by people aiming to show you how things are supposed to be done on the basis of the "authority" vested in them. Such people—relatives, priests, politicians, employers, friends and experts—have been giving us "advice" since the earliest days of our childhood. However, in reality they have been frequently thwarting us and putting us down.

A large number of counseling services have emerged. They thrive on our voluntary relinquishment of our skill at conducting our lives, on the generally prevailing disorientation, on the loss of Self-empowerment and of individual responsibility. We frequently assert that other people are entitled, qualified and authorized to lead us. So go ahead and take advantage of the opportunity now. Begin to live in a Self-reliant manner.

Or perhaps you believe that the advice you get will save you from the ultimate fate of death that each of us faces? And remember one thing: an advisor or counselor hardly ever shows up at a funeral and takes the blame for the death of the person he advised. Usually such "authorities" claim just the opposite: "He only had himself to blame!"

Once all theologians, politicians, legal, tax and financial consultants, social, life and health counselors, dietitians and all psychological, physiological, sexual, respiratory, body and energy therapists have exhausted themselves in giving advice, you will be so full of instructions, tips and good counsel that you will no longer know what to do. However, you may finally realize that it is time to take responsibility for yourself, that it is time to sit down and clear your mind.

Take your life into your own hands! We can assure you of one thing in blissful certainty:

It is a magnificent feeling to be "unteachable," to be full of the innocent "being your-Self."

You are liberated at the moment in which you free yourself of all the instructions and indoctrination you have accumulated.

Self-confidence is simply feeling unknowing again, is realizing that you and only you—and nobody else—can really know about your path and your life. Self-confidence means having confidence in the Self.

We are not hopelessly thrown into the world, but we ARE our world and all worlds. This reality works in and through us.

Non-Thinking

Accept what Is and observe. Increasingly live as the observer, as the one who does not have to judge, who is only a seeing eye, an alert ear, tasting, smelling, feeling and thinking. Be the observer who recognizes and accepts the ultimate house rules—the cosmic order.

We have chosen not to live in anarchy. It is important to note that some rules are necessary if people want to live together in society. Thanks to our intellect, we are capable of recognizing the need for rules of behavior and laws as well as adhering to them, assuming that these regulations make sense. We only have to think of the hideous reigns of terror in human history to realize what blind and uncritical obedience to lawmakers can lead to.

It could happen that you will be loved a bit less when you are so Self-confident. This is the result of how egos behave towards each other. It begins at a very early age. When you are ill, you are given love, or at least sympathy and pity. Conversely, some people are suspicious when you seem to be doing well.

Permit us to pose a question: have others always wanted to joyfully celebrate with you when you were happy and danced, laughed or sang out loudly, when you rejoiced in life? Just the opposite happens sometimes! When you show that you are happy, you sometimes may be treated with suspicion. Skeptical people assume that something must be wrong with you whenever you are joyous. Perhaps people explain your carefree state by imagining that you take drugs or consume alcohol.

Frequently we believe that a person's normal mental state is marked by frustration, trepidation, depression, despondency, discontent, unhappiness and whatever else describes everything caused by hate, envy, greed, jealousy and the feeling of lack.

Nevertheless, or perhaps for this very reason, celebrating faith is the way to practice it. Just to give you a few examples:

Christians are exhorted to "always rejoice" in the Lord. Jews are called upon to joyfully sing their praises of Hashem. Muslims are asked to love and rejoice in the Prophet. Buddhists say joy is our natural state of being.

All people have an intense longing for love, compassion and bliss in the innermost depths of their beings.

These are the values which constitute life. In fact, they are your essence and your birthright! People who express them stand firmly anchored in truth.

Bliss comes from trusting your inner observer, from looking into this Being with an alert, mindful consciousness, and from realizing that you are not separate or alienated from the Oneness.

All people can attain such a state of Being, as the Son of Man proved in his Self-realization! Lao Tzu said in his *Tao Te Ching*: "Emptying the mind of thoughts equals the empty tranquility of Tao." The only thing you need to do is not to think. Master Yaoshan said, "Think of non-thinking."[36] It sounds easier than it really is. But is anything easy?

The bottom line is that everything meditative is "turning to the center of your Being," or centering yourself. In his book, *To Have or To Be*, Erich Fromm makes a distinction. On the one hand, there is wanting to have and having to have in order to be, to have proof of being here in the first place. On the other hand, there is unintentional Beingness. It is the way towards being whole and being once more with the all-encompassing Oneness. This is our original state.

What is it that makes the chanting of birds so en-chanting? When these tones resound in your heart and not in your intellect, then you actually hear what is being revealed by its pure, natural sound. You realize it is a gift from heaven. You are

Non-Thinking

capable of being meditative and simply being—of being the one Self.

We have "unlearned" the way to hear words which are devoid of any meaning. Imagine being once more a child who is not yet able to express himself verbally. In this phase, you hear words like tones. You are aware of the voice, the sound, perhaps even the pitch of the person speaking. However, you don't give any thought to all these impressions. You also do not understand the synonyms and terms which are abstractly strung together. These words are completely empty for a child. In turn, he does not try to interpret it all, to draw conclusions, to analyze the details or to even struggle to comprehend. The sound flows through the child, in the way an adult hears a foreign language that you do not understand. You penetrate the depths of meditation.

This approach is a completely new way for adults to perceive things. You can see that it can lead us far beyond the limitations of the mind.

We almost always restrict ourselves to training our intellectual capabilities and analytical skills. Instead, we should also focus on and practice the pure and clear perception of the sounds that we hear or the sights that we see. We proceed in this manner until we identify with our minds and intellects and until we falsely believe that we are our thoughts.

Thinking is an excellent skill. It is reserved exclusively for people and we are fortunate to be born as creatures endowed with an intellect.

We are able to use words and sign language to communicate with each other. We are capable of accumulating knowledge and experience, of systematizing it, of creating associations between thoughts, and of drawing creative conclusions.

There a test to determine the extent to which people identify with their cognitive abilities, if you dare to do this. If you tell someone with glasses that he does not see very well, the chances are the individual will not be insulted. He or she is aware of having weak eyesight, and will show understanding for your statement.

However, you will probably not be able to tell a person that he cannot think well without personally and deeply offending him. Why do we identify ourselves so strongly with our intellect? There is reason to suspect that people believe that we not only have an intellect, but that we are one with our intellect.

Why do we give our ability to think a greater right to exist than our ability to see? Why should we think our identity is comprised of our thoughts and ideas? We wrack our brains and mull things over and over in our minds, especially at night, a process which is often so insistent and overpowering that we cannot sleep. And sleeplessness apparently happens against our free will.

"It"—the indescribable, indefinable Oneness—sees, hears, tastes, smells and feels us—and thus lives us. In the same way, It thinks us. Sit down by the wayside and remain completely silent for some time. Dispense with the usual chat and gibberish going on in your mind. If your mind enables you to intentionally and deliberately think and to do whatever you want, as you may believe, then you should also be able to command it to let go of thinking at any time. Or perhaps you can't? Refrain from making any daring assertions. Simply try it out and see what happens.

The thinking of abstract thoughts becomes possible only after we learn language and are able to define terms, form concepts, and create synonyms. We then use them to describe a reality or to talk about it. However, such synonyms have nothing in common with reality. Their capabilities are limited to setting up somewhat useful allusions.

Non-Thinking

Our learning to ponder life, to reflect on experiences, and to let actions lag behind our thoughts has caused us to distance ourselves from reality. We also move away from our-Selves whenever this process takes on a life of its own. As a consequence, we become "lost in thought," "not in our right mind," "out of our senses" and "out of it." The more we analyze and dissect the Isness and Suchness, the more we kill our awareness of the wholeness, of Oneness, and of the one Divine Spirit underlying Existence.

This is how the mind normally works. But you are capable of becoming mindful, and of making the mind your servant. Let the mind do its work as best as it can, but be vigilant and on guard that the mind remains what it is—a sensory organ.

That is why the Japanese believe there to be six senses—as opposed to our five. According to them, we see, hear, smell, taste, feel—and think!

In fact, by regarding thinking to be a sense, we have the possibility to go beyond the mind. By doing such, we get the ability to transcend thinking and, at the same time, to develop our mental faculties. Once this has occurred, we will not be as interested in enjoying "mind-boggling" experiences or in "blowing your mind" as in moving beyond this world. It's time for us to courageously put aside our superficial ego-based thinking. It makes us believe we are nothing more than thinkers. We are also "feelers." However, in this case, this term refers to the awareness of pure, clear consciousness and of an all-encompassing Being.

Being simply pleased at having such an instrument at our disposal—such a sixth sense—enables us to employ thinking in a totally different way. Taking this new approach will enable the instrument—our minds—to be allowed to take breaks and to overcome its limits. This will give rise to profound peace and serenity.

Peaceful tranquility exists when our thought processes come to a standstill.

Many of the methods shown to us by masters of meditation are designed to calm the mind and open up a new dimension for us. They lead us to Sat, Chit and Ananda—to Being, Conscious Being and Bliss.

When you are in a state in which names and concepts are no longer necessary, you are free to "become like little children."[37]

WU WEI WU

WHAT SETS US free? Childlike naturalness does, provided that we have yet to be entrapped by the illusion of a fragmented reality, when it is joined by our abiding in clarity of mind and in pureness of spirit. In turn, this permits us to clearly see the path we are on. We are then free to wander in truth.

If something makes you restless and arouses in you the belief that what you have learned is not true, take a closer look at whom or what it is that does not want to accept that thinking. Remember that reflecting, brooding and speculating form minuscule parts of what is possible!

Ever since we learned how to speak and how to make distinctions, the "I" has grown progressively more dominant. This starts in childhood and extends to young adulthood. To use an analogy, the "I"—our ego process—has ripened like fruit on a tree during this time. It is time for you to let this fruit fall to the ground, so that it does not get rotten and poison the tree.

It is an act of grace to be able to recognize freedom and to not be attached to the ego, which is nothing more than a process not rooted in reality. The ego is something that has made itself the center of your attention, something you have allowed to disguise your true Being. You will see how the ego has been limiting you once you are capable of realizing you are much more than all the ideas, images and concepts that you have of yourself.

To accomplish this, you also have to allow darkness in your life. Light requires darkness to shine. In darkness, there is Nobody who can see. Nobody is there to make distinctions, and Nobody is there to wander in darkness or in light.

Everything will be clear once the light of realization appears. It shines in the darkness of non-knowing and non-thinking.

Human beings with an awareness of their origins are capable of transcending their minds. Do this. Once this happens, you will realize that the ego in you, which makes itself more important than the Source and which believes itself to be so helpless, is only a figment of your imagination.

In other words, you will not suffer any losses by letting go of the ego. It was only an image in you, a concept of yourself conveyed to you by all the mirrors in the world. It was something you took at face value. Go and search for what you really are. Find what you were before all the education and upbringing made you so self-important—as opposed to Self-important. Return to your inherent nature, the one extant prior to all the ideas and concepts which took over and put themselves in the forefront of your life.

The principle of Wu Wei Wu—"doing by not doing"—is a fundamental principle of Chinese Taoism. This philosophy complemented its teaching with aspects of Buddhism and Confucianism. They all mutually enriched each other. The teachings of Chan or Zen view all of Existence as being infused with the one Spirit. They thus go above and beyond the ways of thinking inherent in the above three religious movements. Bodhidharma (Ta-Mo), the founder of Zen in China, was joined by Sosan, Hui Neng, Rinzai and the true Masters of all spiritual schools in revealing to us the "non-doing" in their doing. This requires our belief in the language of their hearts. These masters let go of their ego processes and became distinguished Nobodies.

Remarkable Nobodies! If such a Nobody does something, then Nobody does anything, and non-doing arises. This entails acting without intention. This is real doing by not doing. We are reminded of the unintentional, unconstrained laughter of the Chinese. Laughing in such a way is an exercise practiced in Qi Gong. There is no doer to do anything, and notwithstanding this, things are done well.

It is the doing that is naturally being done. A matter of natural course is that nothing with a sense of purpose then arises.

When we do what comes from our very (divine) nature, our inner Being, we no longer differentiate and distinguish. Instead, we live in the awareness of never having been separated from our own nature.

All suffering and pain come from our separating, distinguishing and distancing ourselves, so as to exist in a state of duality. That is why these differences are buried in the graveyard of all vanities, desires and the ego! Thinking divides, distinguishes and separates us. It is the basis for our seeming to be apart from the Oneness. We are stuck in the dualism between good and evil. This places us as far away from the truth as Heaven is from Earth.

We are intact, holy and divine in the wholeness.

You will be able to let go and experience serenity and tranquility once you allow life to remain a mystery. By doing such, you will be able to accept the wholeness and Oneness of life and of its being unfathomable and unsolvable.

You can let go by allowing yourself to accept It as the truth and by letting It unfold in you. At this very moment, you ARE the all-encompassing everything.

Your consciousness encompasses the entire cosmos!

Whenever you think in terms of duality, whenever you focus on the "good," you create "evil." If you see yourself as being "high," there is also a "low." Should you proceed with this, you will experience yourself to be either the one causing suffering or the one perceiving it.

Who is the one to experience himself or herself in this manner?

All divisions disappear once you stop making distinctions, once everything becomes One and whole. If you perceive no winner, there is also no loser. The winner who separates himself from the loser due to his identification with winning ultimately also ends up losing.

Nobody is making the claim that our hand wants to live in a way separating it from the rest of our body. Our hand does not claim to have its own identity. It would be completely lost without the rest of the organism, and would soon go numb and die without a blood supply or nerves.

One fundamental mistake often made by us is to see ourselves as being placed helplessly in the middle of Existence. We fail to perceive ourselves as being part of the cosmos, without which we would not be able to survive in the first place. This is due to our state of unconsciousness and to false interpretations of religion. The latter stop people from being whole and "striking it rich" in their search for truth. As mentioned before, "religare" (religion) means to reconnect to your inner being, to find yourself again in the Oneness of the one Spirit, the All-One. This takes place when you "don't mind" whatever happens and can embody equanimity.

So what is it that has prevented us from making these discoveries? Who immediately asks: "What?"

Let us repeat something here: The ego process excessively overestimates itself. It isolates itself from others. It is the source of disunity and of disconnection. It causes suffering, and also suffers itself. It is the embodiment of arrogance. The ego seems to be appropriate to us, although in fact it is a made-to-measure suit that completely restricts our movement, and which is actually imposed upon us. Notwithstanding this, we still identify with it. This is what Buddha was referring to when he stated that "life is suffering."

People sacrifice contentment, happiness and their physical and emotional health on behalf of and to satisfy their egos.

Our attempts to maintain this glow of success and to pursue the seemingly endless process of deliberately doing things leaves us hopelessly overburdened, collectively stressed, tormented and sick. We do work nobody wants or needs, work which makes us and other people suffer.

We even forget the possibility of partaking of the highest realization there is—that we can enjoy grace without having to do anything for it. You cannot "earn" or "deserve" grace.

Should we have to do something to receive grace, we would not be children of God. We would not be unconditional and the Kingdom of God would not be in us.

Wu Wei Wu.

Simply try not to do anything. But still nothing remains undone!

THE TRANQUIL FLOW

Moving between dualisms is moving in harmony with the flow of life. This unfolds the same way as a leaf does on the river. It floats along, riding on the flow of life. While playfully being carried along, the leaf lets go and surrenders to the flow. It moves with unbelievable certainty towards the ocean.

This ocean can be found in Qi Gong, and in practicing "life care," the style of practice which is called "Yangsheng" in Chinese. This means "nourishing life." This ocean is also cited in Qi Hai, an acupuncture point below the navel, in the interior of the abdomen, but more importantly, it nourishes the sea of Qi (Chi) or the center of the energy of life. You will feel yourself linked once again to the energy of life at the very moment you let go to be in the flow and yield to it, when you allow the "Suchness" to be. The flow carries you and you move with it. You do not get tired and are blissful because it flows through you and pervades you. It comfortingly nourishes, strengthens, enriches and heals you infinitely and eternally.

You are able to perceive that you are in harmony with the cosmos. You realize that you have always been in this state, because you carry the divine life in you, and you ARE divine.

You are also "the way, the truth and the life."[38]

Jesus of Nazareth, called the Son of Man, is also the Son of God in a very natural way, as we are all children of God. In the Orient, people often use quite figurative language. For instance, they are prone to call a man the "Son of the Desert," the "Son of the Sun" and similar things.

A person speaking from a state of enlightenment utters truth directly. The compassion flowing through him enables Self-realization to be radiated in manifold ways. This provides the people encountering him with a wide variety of approaches to the truth. Jesus speaks about being "in the world but not of the world."[39] He is thus calling out to the observer in us. This observer is alert and independent, regarding matters without judging, serving as a witness seeing with unclouded eyes.

Now that you are firmly anchored in the truth, no single thing and no person can lead you astray. You finally know who flows with the Tao. The expression of "I AM THAT I AM" is attributed to God in the Old Testament.[40] The authority and credibility of these words are to be discovered in the Self-awareness of the Masters, who through the ages have awakened to their true essence.

The mastery attained by such true leaders was often frequently questioned, even contested. This was due to their not belonging to a certain religion—or to having liberated themselves from dependencies, affiliations and organizations.

It is rare that an "anti-guru" can convincingly demonstrate that she or he is independent of any connection to a religion or denomination. Such persons may in fact belong to a religious institution, association or party. Such leaders often have nothing else in mind than taking possession of people to further establish their "profundities" and to advance their interests. They often aim to exploit people for the purpose of taking advantage of opportunities to demonstrate their power and dictate our spirituality.

Do your work. Eat. Drink. Sleep. But do not allow yourself to be fooled by false prophets.

Be imbued with the truth on the basis of your clear awareness.

The Middle Way transcends all opposites and paradoxes. This powerful awareness was realized on the path taken by the wise Buddha five centuries before Christ. Buddha did not arrive at enlightenment by living extremely ascetically—or through self-mortification. Rather, living in a strictly ascetic manner, Buddha's complete exhaustion caused him to fall into the Ganges. The Buddha had to be rescued. This experience caused him to realize that there was absolutely no point in weakening and humiliating himself, or wearing himself out physically and mentally. Who else could he help if he could not even save himself?

The Middle Way does not demand that we push ourselves to the limit. Those who do so are victims of their egos, which asks: why not simply force your way to enlightenment? The answer: because it is impossible! You cannot force your way into the Kingdom of God. Anyone who seeks enlightenment will never attain it. Buddha did not become enlightened through his spending long nights immersed in meditation under the Bodhi tree, which was an act of doing. Being blessed with grace came to him after he had fallen asleep and had woken up the next morning. The Buddha looked up and saw the morning star shining in the sky. The grace that he experienced had arisen from his having let go, letting things take their course, and from a gracious and merciful serenity.

You are entitled to draw your own conclusions from this story. Apply it to witness the strengthening of the power within you, a strengthening caused by your dwelling in the harmony lying between the two poles of opposition. This causes the poles to dissipate and your situation is resolved. This sets you free. Let yourself be inspired in this state of being released, by feeling your health and inner peace. In this way you are fulfilled in wholeness. You are living a wonderful state of emptiness. All forms and everything new are born from emptiness.

It is written in the Heart Sutra that "form is emptiness and emptiness is form." This teaching wants to show us that everything that exists, all phenomena, whether scientifically proved or not, requires nothingness or emptiness to do so. This enjoyable fullness is made possible by the interplay of these two polarities.

You are capable of experiencing bliss, of being bliss in infinite, boundless Being, in enlightened, empty consciousness. This state lacks content, and is thus capable of embodying the Divine.

"Wonderful, how wonderful is the tranquil flow of the indescribable Tao."

Tao—"the Way"—is the cosmos, the universe, Existence, the Self! Can one describe Tao in any other way except as "indescribable" and "wonderful," to use Lao Tzu's words?

Is it also not true, as Lao Tzu said, that "He who knows, does not speak. He who speaks, does not know"? We have already said far too much here. Perhaps you have the feeling that we seem to be saying the same thing over and over again. Perhaps you are getting tired of this. Well, this is not surprising. You have always had all of this wisdom in you. Now that you are finally hearing the solution, you want to get quick results and come to a conclusion.

All this will not be handed to you on a plate, neither in this book nor anywhere else! Our objective is to find a variety of ways to express the same thing, in order to empower you to unfold what is inside of you. We are sparing no effort, so we use lurid colors to paint this picture and to jangle you with dissonant chords. All this is being done so that you may see the impossible as a possibility. We are doing everything in our power to describe the indescribable in words that make sense to you.

Once you have accepted this, the next step is to give up always trying to understand everything. Thinking and thoughts become boring.

It would be OK for you to put down the book in boredom. Thoroughly enjoy this feeling. If we never have time for anything, then we literally do not have any life-time. Therefore, we humbly accept boredom as a gift of the moment. On the other hand, if reading this book has been helpful, then perhaps you should continue reading.

You ARE and exist in the state of boredom which has been given to us.

You are now aware that the sense of it all displays itself and unfolds without our having to prompt it. Now it is time to recall the wisdom of a Master, who replied to the question about the meaning of life by posing another question: "How does green taste?" Allow this puzzle to melt on your tongue, swallow it and let it work in you until you have digested and absorbed it. It will nourish your life and make you rich in spirit.

There is nothing but the one Spirit.

"There is really no truth to be understood. You do not have to seek understanding. Truth is nothing that needs to be proved."

—Ta-Mo

THE WAY TO PERFECTION

"Why do you concern yourself with the judgments of others? Why should a fish in the depths of a lake be concerned about whether or not a fisherman likes him?"

—Ta-Mo

WE HAVE BEEN wandering around for some time now. It was not difficult for you to realize that the path we have been traveling on is pathless. How can you ask for certainty once you realize that it is pathless? How can we make any guarantees concerning the direction we are moving in? It is not intellectual knowledge that leads us and enables us to make progress. Our hearts are what we use to discern things.

Take your walking stick and hit the ground with it. Then try to tell other people what you hear when it hits the ground and what its vibrations convey. All aspects of these tremors and the experience of sound cannot be conveyed by any terms and concepts, no matter how sophisticated they may be.

People are even less capable of conveying truth in words. We cannot express the ultimate realization or awareness that we are struggling to apprehend. We have no words capable of denoting this deep-seated longing which pushes us forward and compels us to continue searching. The use of a diverse range of concepts, each with many syllables, won't change the bottom line that words are uncommunicative and limited. They are never able to convey even a tiny smattering of what reality really is.

All philosophies only show us the impotence of words.

The use of words to describe true realization or awareness fails due to a simple fact: words are basically meaningless.

When you do not try to supply names for the truth, everything lingers in namelessness. Our mind is very suspicious of this, as it offers no certainty. But show us something providing any certainty at all. Show us something able to define, codify and secure life.

Believe in life's uncertainty and insecurity, which characterizes life as it really is. For those giving life names: be aware that life does not allow itself to be labeled or designated. Lao-Tzu appropriately told us that the Tao is not nameable.

The path of meditation is not a topic for rational debate or intellectual banter. Let's not engage in any discussions! The realization of the Highest is deeply concealed in you and would be limited if it could be named.

Thus, be happy that you are infinite, boundless, nameless limitlessness. Laugh about how we limit ourselves whenever we try to restrict our Self. This need causes people to go as far as to have their achievements or possessions engraved on their tombstones—by way of an example: "Professor Dr. Anna Burger, home owner."

We appreciate the fact that possessions often mean something to their owners. We understand that they distinguished the dead person when she was alive. However, being dead means she cannot take her possessions with her, not even the proverbial "shirt on her back." The description she used calls attention to her status as someone who was successful and rich. Its ultimate thrust is to reduce her to a material level. We diminish ourselves—even in death—by invoking property, status and knowledge. Instead, we should focus on spiritual values and the very basis for Existence.

What happens if you do not classify yourself or allow yourself to be put in a professional- or activity-oriented straitjacket? Then you will have the following words put on your tombstone to more or less describe the role you played in life: "Here is the resting place for what is mortal in people."

Instead of embracing this reality, we voluntarily diminish ourselves. We do this out of love for and bondage to our egos. Instead of focusing on our infinite and endless divine nature, we emphasize the nothingness, for example, of being a senior government official. We display the roles that we played in life as the proud emblems and flagships of our uniqueness.

However, we succeed in achieving just the opposite of what we intended. We make ourselves into a worm, instead of becoming one with the endless ocean of Cosmic Being. Not to mention the fact that we will be stepped upon when lying in our graves. The worm is capable of being mistreated and insulted and is forced to bend down in obedience. This is an unworthy and disgraceful way to make the most of our inherent potential.

Accept namelessness, and seek to attain your original state.

Everything and anything comes together in and goes back to the One. But where does this One go back to? To pose this question, we invoke this powerful koan, which is an almost unsolvable mystery. Oneness is also indescribable and unexplainable. Buddha spoke in this regard of "not two" or non-duality. Say that you have studied medicine, or became a priest, or held political office, or became an executive or top manager, or whatever else you think you are. Our question for you is: who is it identifying with this role at this very moment? Who dreams this dream? How would you describe a perception based on something which does not exist?

Do you not know or do you not want to know that you are only dreaming and that you are playing these roles in your dream? And you do so for a limited time only, because the dream is temporary. You play the role only marginally well and with limited success.

Find the player! Recognize the dreamer!

Don't talk about which roles the actor or actress already played. Nobody is interested. Do not try to explain to us what roles he will play in the future, which roles he learned, for which venues he has been asked to play, how well he performed—or will perform. And don't tell us how nervous he was before the last premiere and which concepts are behind his acting.

Show us who the playing dreamer or the dreaming player is between the closing and opening of your eyelids! The answer is concealed in the moment between these two blinks of an eye. It is always there at the moment and here at the present time, and thus seemingly hidden. It has always been there and will always be there, but is capable of being grasped only in the here and now. There is nothing to think about, describe or hold on to.

It is life itself which is so fleeting. It flees from you like love does when you are attached to it, try to pin it down and hold on to, own or try to analyze it.

Learn through and from this emptiness. And then teach all people the perception of what really is.

First learn to empty yourself. Teaching from emptiness means drawing upon infinite abundance.

Life breathes, pulsates and lives you, just as breathing fills you when you breathe in and empties you when you breathe out. The same applies to life. It fills you at supposed birth and empties you at supposed death. Life lives you in the same way that the closing of your eyelids voids you of visual impressions, and the opening of your eyes fills you with the beauty of colors and forms.

If you want to get a glimpse of how nameless thinking works, do exercises from the Chinese practice of Qi Gong. Let yourself be carried and fulfilled, opened, expanded and imbued by breath. This causes Chi, the universal life energy, to flow through you, to pulsate like a huge, powerful current. Breathe and be fulfilled far down in the depths of your being, and you will experience and live it.

Deciding to go against the flow of life and swim against nature will consume all your strength, and you will go limp and drown in the floods of the universe. The universe does not show any concern for you. Lot's wife in the Bible was not the only one who looked back and was turned into a salt pillar. Whoever is not for God, the Source, the Oneness, pits herself or himself against it. Whoever is not for himself and his life and who does not flow with life will soon solidify in death. Let the dead bury their own dead![41]

Creation itself does not make any mistakes. The universe will be incomprehensible for you should you spend your time tormenting yourself and bogged down in thought. It will also be this way when your mind is filled to the brim with problems. The universe has no compassion for the inability to keep a cool head, breathe freely or sleep soundly, or to not stop a steadily escalating symphony of thoughts. The universe does not stop in its tracks and turn inwards in order to pity you or feel sympathy for you because you are suffering so much from your self-imposed isolation and alienation.

Existence itself will teach you to observe how the birds continue to sing despite difficulties you may experience. Existence has ways to lift your spirit. It shows you the flowers blossoming and the shining of the sun on a wonderful morning.

It might be helpful to know that your neighbor may not understand why you celebrate life with love, laughing and dancing. He or she can deal much better with the suffering that torments so many people. It is the same pattern of behavior we experienced and learned when we were brought up. We prefer to suffer or indulge in the suffering of others instead of rejoicing.

It is as if we enjoy resigning ourselves to some higher power, trying to please it, and feeling that we are not up to the task and cannot meet its demands. That is why we draw attention to our suffering and the pain we still feel. The pain is what stops us from proceeding with our "education" and from being fully responsible for our actions. The pain wants us to act like little children recovering from an illness.

Notwithstanding this, there is no need for us to comply with any power. No harm is done by our belonging to our-Selves and trusting it. Having confidence in the Self is true Self-confidence. You are capable of getting there, and, once you arrive, of rejoicing like a fish does about the water in which it swims. You will be able to fully and truly partake of life. You are this life. It is everything that you "have." You are everything and everything is in you.

> "Teaching means distributing medicine tailored to the illness. When there is thunder in the sky, there is an echo. It acts in the same way."
>
> —Ta-Mo

WITHOUT SEEKING

The path continues over the mountain and through the valley. As we proceed along it, we observe the miracles that this landscape manifests! Let us imbibe the beauty and powerful perseverance of the water which flows in the valley while on its way to the ocean. It manages this feat even when encountering the hardest rock. The water keeps on breaking ground and conveying deep pearls of wisdom to us. Water is the strongest force. It moves without intention and resistance, yields when necessary, acts flexibly and mildly, and nourishes existing and new life. Water's strength comes from going with the flow instead of resisting it.

Whenever there is nothing there that needs to be understood, whenever no names need to be given, then there is also Nobody who needs to understand, to hand out names or to get an impression of anything.

The indefinable form of the cosmos is reflected in the originally empty state of Being.

Being is the state of clear consciousness and awareness. In this state you are imbued with the Oneness, are no longer separated, and experience yourself as being one with the One Source.

This "wholeness" is an expression of the all-encompassing love that the Masters who have come before us manifested. You will embrace it at the moment when, while in the state of emptiness—which is really a state of abundance—you recognize yourself in everything. We thrive when we are in the infinite space, instead of being in the large number of limiting "forms" to which we were attached. The universe works in and through you when you no longer hold onto life through your ego, when life flows through you, and when you embody your divine dimension. The emptiness in you, which is what you really are, is realized and expressed.

Upon its having happened, you are that which can say, "I AM THAT I AM." There is absolutely no difference, no separation. Everything is in you and you are in everything. There is no "separate" seeker, in fact there never was a seeker at all, but only Being—conscious Beingness, instead of separation, of being separated from yourself. Indeed this is truly bliss.

Water flows downwards through the valley, into the lowlands and always towards the sea. There is an abundance of symbols in the "sacred" texts that explain how the highest points can be reached by their being part of the depths of creation. One example is the parable of the lotus blossom, which has its roots in the mud. The lotus rises from the mud to emerge as the most splendid blossom around. It particularly thrives in the clearest and most brilliant sunlight. The pearl of wisdom of a Chinese Master is very instructive here:

"If the branches of a tree want to rise as far up as heaven, the roots have to extend down into hell."

Communicate with all sentient beings through love and compassion. Your base for doing such is in coming to terms with all the egoism and attributes of your "I," with accepting them and yourself as you are in the here-now. Nothing separates us except false perceptions. Free yourself from all the beliefs and concepts in which you wrongly believe you exist as an island unto yourself, isolated from all that is human.

However, if you continue to nourish the ego, it will drain you of all your energy and happiness. At some point, you will come to dread the hardship of continually propping up an edifice that is built upon fragile pillars and of patching it in order to prevent it from falling apart. A house made of cards cannot stand.

Finding without seeking takes place by having our consciousness cleared up by the process of grace. Through it, we are able to be inspired by our bond and affinity to the Oneness, and by the blessing granted to us, to recognize the underlying undividedness of everything.

The Tao Te Ching conveys the message to us to not be attached to the abundance and fullness we may experience, but to let go instead: "A house filled with riches cannot be defended." Pride in one's prosperity and reputation is both an illusion and deception. This will become apparent when they are illuminated by the light of immeasurable Being. When that happens, you will not be able to save the dwelling and its wealth of vanities. Your income and the possessions that you love to show off and the status you derive from them only lead to reducing yourself—as opposed to becoming aware of what you really are.

"The Great Way has no gate, and is pathless. So what is the way?"[42]

The Way is not something visible. Nor are our senses capable of perceiving it. Despite this, the path is not invisible but perceptible. Should it not be, wise beings from all eras of human history would not have been able to relate it to you. So let us travel along the pathless path, to the extent possible.

The Way is not something tangible and comprehensible. Conversely, it is also not incomprehensible either. That is why we find it without seeking it. We do not teach the Way, and you do not learn it, but we are on it, and while on it, we are completely open and vast like the endless sky.

Become like the white clouds. They always find the Way without seeking.

A seeming dichotomy has revealed itself to you. On one side of the gulf, there are the questionable, deeply human heights of the ego. On the other, there is the uncertainty, namely the world of the Absolute, which is elusive to our human understanding. On the one hand, there is the well-known and well-beaten egocentric path of contemplating your navel—spending an overly large amount of time focusing on yourself and your problems. On the other hand, there is the unimaginable and indefinable state of mindlessness and ego-lessness. Are you capable of making the decision as to which you prefer?

Be indiscriminateness itself.

BE SERENE

Each of us has experienced in our own very personal way what it means to be out of tune with our inner harmony due to greed, hate, envy, jealousy and all the other "blossoms" of the ego. Every person who fails to realize what happens to him through insisting upon being Somebody, being an "individual," has to bear the negative consequences.

It is impossible for the ego to remain a Nobody. With this commencing at the moment of our birth, we are conditioned, trained and educated to acquire knowledge and skills for use in successfully competing in the jungle of the outside world. Something to be remembered is that the blade of any knife becomes dull when you hold it too intensely onto the sharpening stone.

To have an overabundance of things, to know and be esteemed as much as possible are what the ego strives for in its lust for self-preservation. It is willing to do anything to achieve these goals, even though the efforts may result in the loss of our lives. So employ your mindfulness whenever you feel an ambition to live according to these values. Remember that this ambition will lead (and mislead) you into believing the goals are viable and doable, and that attaining them will enable you to achieve supposed happiness and questionable satisfaction.

The problem with this thinking is that once you reach these objectives, you have to engage in a fight—a hopeless one—to hold on to them. This drains you of all of your energy.

Possessions do not make you richer, but they do make you busier! Striving for power and profit keeps you imprisoned in your blindness. It also holds you back from seeking the seeker.

We are not talking at all about doing without possessions, or about giving up on the joys of life, or about withdrawing from life or even living passively. We are talking about taking a new look at a life now being spent pursuing material wealth and prestige. The bottom line is that you can have everything you want or already own provided that you do not identify with these things. Do not make the mistake of believing that you are these mountains of rubbish. They cost you precious time and quality of life. This sacrifice can never be compensated by hard cash or social status. The bottom line is that neither the treadmill of life—the rat race—nor the attachment to the ego nor the belief in duality can bring you fulfillment. The pursuit of your current way of living will cause you to sing the famous anthem of the Rolling Stones, "I Can't Get No Satisfaction."

End-of-life care for the dying has taught us that the one regret that people with a short time left to live mainly suffer from is the feeling that they never really lived life at all. They regret a life of having been perpetually busy, of collecting things, of struggling and striving to satisfy the obsession with wanting to "have." And only at the very end, in the last days of their lives, do they realize that these actions were all forlorn hopes and vain endeavors. Looking back, they wish instead that they had focused on "being."

Jesus said: "My kingdom is not of this world."[43] If you accumulate possessions and fail to learn to let go, then death, the ultimate teacher, will quickly change your mind. Death will empty you of everything you were so proud of, everything for which you sacrificed your happiness in life, your lifetime and joy.

Only when you finally realize that nothing at all can really belong to you—no object or sentient being, not even your children—will you feel that there is nothing for you to let go of. If nothing ever really belongs to you, there is nothing for you to lose. You can stop surrounding yourself with all those seemingly important things. You can let go of them and be serene.

Don't we seem to engage in a never-ending process of stuffing ourselves with new contents and developing attachments to new forms, so that we have even bigger problems to face?

Let us bravely empty our pockets and abide in a deep, serene and unperturbed state of Being.

This will cause the light to increasingly shine in you. You will feel your innate strength and will increasingly embody love. Praise will no longer be required to keep your spirits high and to keep you standing tall. Criticism will no longer be able to humiliate you and put you down. There is Nobody to be put on a pedestal, and Nobody to be dragged down to the depths of agony. You will sit in silence and your spirit will aimlessly abide in namelessness itself. Questions that plagued you will dissipate. You no longer require answers.

Hear the song of the crickets!

Return to observing. We let our breath come and go. Observe your spine. See how it slightly straightens up when you breathe in, just like a cobra does when it wishes to survey the scene, and slackens when you breathe out. Your body slumps a little before stretching out again. Enjoy the game of taking and giving. Know that "the energy of life rides on the dragon of breath."[44] You fill and empty yourself as the law commands.

Please understand what we mean by "law." We do not mean a law imposed upon us from the outside. Such laws limit, mangle, maul and bind us. We do mean a law of Nature itself, one that you can understand without thinking—as it is entirely and implicitly natural.

Look at a cat waiting patiently in front of the mouse hole. It is lying there fully relaxed. It would seem to be sleeping; however, it is actually wide awake. Otherwise it would be unable to catch the mouse when it comes out of its hiding place. The cat's muscles are apparently relaxed to the point of somnolence. They are actually ready to pounce! The cat is at the highest level of mindfulness. The cat is not "lost in thought." It does not reflect and dwell about the past, nor does it indulge in lust for the male cat. The cat and all its senses are completely in the present.

Our letting go enables us to resort to the relaxation technique of imagining ice melting in the cells of our body, allowing it to drip out of all the pores in our skin. This makes it possible for us to let go of ourselves more deeply, to surrender to and trust in gravity. Upon doing such, you are precisely in the same mental and physical condition as the cat. You can reach such a high level of serenity by being open, porous, serene, unhurried, satisfied, fully relaxed and yet vibrant and full of playful and pulsating energy.

Grace teaches you at this moment that the impermanent is permanent. What is immutable and unchanging is the constant flux of all things. Now that you are grounded in a deep sense of humility and equanimity, you can see how unchangeable constant change is. It is within everything that is natural.

By way of contrast to this naturalness, being outside it means being superficial or "man-made," being alienated from what is natural. It means deviating from the path. "The straight line is a godless line!"[45] This saying expresses the fact that linear thinking, straight lines and categorizing things may seem to you to be the logical and reliable way to proceed. However, this way of living causes us to lose our connection to the natural.

We are much more than we can ever make of ourselves.

Many people pursue the goal of ultimately becoming "children of God." Based on this arrogant human presumption, people push aside humility and to try to make the divine being we already are into a "child of God." Instead of achieving this, these people actually accomplish a further feeding of their eternally hungry egos. Such people mistakenly believe that all types of measures are required to be undertaken to lift them to the point that they "deserve" to be children of God.

A sculptor is capable of causing a stone to reveal what is already inherently in it. His job is to "merely" chip away all that is unnecessary. Similarly, you will find the light in yourself once you realize that you cannot be anyone or anything else than who or what you already are. There is nothing you can add. You only have to let it be, regardless of the burdens you think you carry on your shoulders, the mask you wear over your face, the clothes you wear, and the particular role in life you play.

Eternity is characterized by the fact that it cannot be destroyed. Neither you nor anyone else in the universe is capable of extinguishing the external light. Similarly, each one of us is unconditional and one with the Oneness, a fact which cannot be changed by any action or thought process on the part of human beings.

> "How could the sun and moon not shine on all the phenomena that appear? How could it all not be brightly illuminated if one holds up a light?"
>
> —Ta-Mo

QUITE SIMPLE

HAVE YOU EVER noticed that even though the world is continually being improved, such improvements do not make it a better place to live afterwards? Something interesting: people assume that a Master does not make mistakes, that she or he is infallible and perfect. I, Genro, can guarantee you that I have never met a true Master who claimed to be perfect. A true Master also neither claims nor attempts to profit from such a supposed perfection. How true and wonderful it is to know that one is entitled to be the most perfectly imperfect being!

Let us try to work out what perfection means for a person. Have we not had enough of those who use their supposed "perfection" to try to continually improve, train, toughen up and perfect others? The alleged benefactions and blessings imposed by such "perfect beings" upon their followers frequently bring utter disaster to them.

Why do you think it is so difficult for you to let go and simply be where you already are? You know why! Because someone repeatedly told you that you have to "change for the better" and develop yourself personally before you could be successful, find happiness and be satisfied. People exist and move around in this breeding ground of continually striving to get somewhere, of having to do more, have more, achieve more and be more in order to "add value" to their lives.

These self-proclaimed "infallible" pseudo-gurus keep people away from seeking the truth. This is a terrible kind of wrongdoing.

Let us take this a step further. Could you imagine that there would be no reason to require an intermediary between us and ultimate truth? No reason to need the—artificially created—fear of purgatory, hell, death and the devil? Truth can only be directly experienced. It is impossible to grasp truth by calling upon an institutionalized intermediary. Institutions and individuals on the outside may serve us as guides or signposts, but sooner or later you yourself have to delve directly and deeply into yourself to discover what you really are.

Ultimately, even though they provide us with a measure of assistance at some point in our lives, the fact is that we can do without all the propagated rituals, intermediaries, teachers, spiritual methods and meditative techniques. All these activities are part of the relative world. These activities are mostly comprised of empty chatter and of mumbo-jumbo. They do not enable you to unfold your true Being.

One guru from India developed dozens of rules for people to follow to gain enlightenment. The rules included refraining from the consumption of alcohol, coffee, meat and cigarettes; of getting up very early to meditate; of abstaining almost completely from sex, and of observing periods of not speaking every day and so on. Some of these actions may be good in themselves for a variety of reasons. However, as one sage wisely said: "It is not important what goes in but what comes out of you. The key is what you express, what you unfold in your-Self, what you ARE."

The Self Is.

This process of unfolding may even require us to leave companions behind. This is what is meant by the saying "If you meet the Buddha, kill him." That is why you "leave the boat behind when you reach the other shore," as Buddha stated. Other sayings are "one throws away the fish nets when the fish are caught" or "you get rid of the crutches when you can walk again." In other words, when you reach this point, you will be capable of leaving behind your ego, former life, denial of the Self, and concepts and dependencies and attachments to our material world. You will also be capable of leaving behind your dependence on so-called "spiritual" practices.

In our enlightened day and age, science is providing increasing evidence that primeval religions, old Masters and wise contemporaries are right when they say:

Be moderate in everything you do, and return to what is simple and natural.

We are by no means talking about becoming ascetic or asexual, or denying the joys in life, or becoming passive or indifferent. What we do mean by "returning to what is simple and natural" is for you to become aware of the workings of the egoistic process by turning to the core of your inner Being. Once you have done so, once you are at home in the Oneness, you will not have to search anymore—or do anything except what is natural. You will have found your way home again to the one universal spirit.

There is a story about a Zen Master who arrived one day to view a Zen garden cared for by hard-working monks who were his pupils. They had removed all the autumn leaves to please him by creating something perfect. Rather than praising the monks, he scattered withered leaves on the path—to the astonishment of the pupils-. The Master did this because he knew it would be unnatural not to have such leaves. Perfection is not natural. As we learned above, the straight line is a godless line.

The perfection of Existence naturally makes imperfection perfect.

Do you really believe that enlightenment will make you a faultless person, someone who is ultimately suited to play the role of an infallible human being? Be thankful that this is not the case. However, enlightenment does do something very important. It illuminates the darkness in which we previously moved.

Everything makes an appearance from the one, undivided, clear and pure Self and ultimately returns to the Self.

In the course of time, some religious organizations may fizzle out and lose popularity. If this does happen, mankind will not lose anything valuable. On the contrary, the disappearance of such religions may cause humanity to experience a truthful and spiritual renaissance and a new zest to seek and find.

Don't let the withered relics being brandished by established religions intimidate you. Have no fear about whether good or evil will survive. We know that good cannot exist without evil and vice versa.

The path to truth, life and the Self is a freely-flowing one. It moves, adapts, undermines and sweeps away rigid forms and institutions. You know this feeling. It is the pure, clear awareness that awaits when you wake up in the morning. Where was it when you slept deeply? During the unconsciousness of sleep, you do not doubt your Being, but are certain of life in a marvelous way. Whilst sleeping, you dwell in both clear and pure consciousness as well as deep unconsciousness.

The Self Is. An unenlightened person is mainly states of mind and perceptions.

TRUE OR NOT TRUE?

Are you sure that we know where we are headed? By undertaking this journey on the pathless path with us, you have placed your trust in us. You trust us to make this journey easier and quicker, whatever and wherever its final destination may be.

Let us frankly confess that we do not know what this destination is! Does the water know where it is going? Doesn't it nevertheless always find its way back to the ocean? Wouldn't it therefore be foolhardy to say that we know something? Isn't it true that we have learned from Socrates that we only know that we know nothing?

Haven't you already been given such an extensive and mass of "knowledge" and instructions from experts, authorities, scholars and pundits telling you the way things are? Haven't you been constantly provided with answers to your most urgent questions? And finally, has all the knowledge and counseling taken you to where you want to be?

Alexander the Great had himself buried with his hands outside the coffin. He aimed to show his warriors that even he who had conquered a huge portion of the world was carried to his grave without any worldly possessions.[46]

In your life, you can accumulate impressive amounts of knowledge. You can learn the telephone book by heart, although computers can do that better. You can (and some readers will have done this) complete a degree at a university. You will thus be bristling with knowledge. Despite this, you will still be at the very place about which Faust complained at the beginning of Goethe's monumental work: "And here, poor fool! With all my lore, I stand no wiser than before!"[47]

In turn, this education may well enable you to get a job with a great deal of status. You may well take pride in your "reputation." The long-term consequences of this may be a close identification with your work. Upon taking your "well-deserved retirement," this could cause you to experience difficulties in adjusting to retired life. The shock that you might experience could even cost you your health. The point of this is: any time that you assume that you are extraordinary and exceptional due to your knowledge and status or other "treasures" that you have accumulated, you will suffer when they are taken away from you.

Liberation from all suffering means taking the path to remember how to be disengaged and detached. You have to let go of all your attachments and dependencies during your lifetime and become fully aware. You may now be able to understand that you cannot add anything or take away anything from what you are. You are already whole and divine.

The purpose of life is fulfilled without our intervention.

We welcome your joining us. Prior to doing such, please allow us to point out that we offer no certainties. It would be amiss for us to claim such, because there is no certainty in the flow of life. The only knowledge helping us in this state of uncertainty is knowing that we are unknowing.

The mind leads us to believe we have ways to solve the mysteries of life, much as if life were a crossword puzzle.

However, a mystery is far from being a puzzle! Imagine that science or technology, medicine or even a religion managed the impossible and deciphered the ultimate puzzle of life. What would there still be left for us to do? We would complain that our task, our calling, our mission and the meaning of life were meaningless.

The bottom line for us is to trust the mysterious aspects of Existence, which cannot be understood by anyone. Nor can it be explained by reason or intellectual skills. The only thing to be done is to simply accept knowing that you ultimately do not and cannot know.

Responding to the question, "Does God exist?" which was posed by someone attached to the idea that there must be a God, Buddha replied: "No, there is no God." The Buddha's teaching was based upon triggering uncertainty in his followers, forcing the pupil to be confronted with reasonable doubts.

Buddha accordingly instructed another pupil who claimed that his beliefs told him that there is no God: "You are mistaken. God exists. Start your quest!" The resulting uncertainties caused the pupil to be thrown back on the path, to be inspired to delve deep and confront his doubts. As a result, he had another opportunity to make a new start to get to know himself and to recognize his Self.

There is something deep in our inner Being that resolves all questions.

If you are courageous, surrender and devote yourself to this search; there is the possibility that not only the question but also the questioning and the questioner will dissolve into nothingness. You will assume a "formless form."

Trust the mystery of Life!

Indra, a Hindu god known for his net, is a symbol of the opposites and concepts designed to explain the absence of concepts.[48] The fusion of these mirror images in the mirrors, which is unimaginable to us, results in the non-conceptual chaos symbolized by Buddha's "non-Self." As is always the case, the explanations of what is inexplicable send the seeker on the detour of vainly pursuing a forlorn hope to explain things. After these attempts have ceased, what is left is only an image of Tao, which is indescribable and inexpressible.

If you, the wanderer on the pathless path, want to go beyond concepts and the lack of concepts, beyond Being and Non-Being, then pose the following questions: what is it that exists, and what existed before all these ideas emerged? What is it that tirelessly tries to explain what is inexplicable? Perceiving this comes before all appearances arose. Existence's origins and roots are inconceivable.

The only time that the Self experiences itself in a sole way is in meditation, in which it is unburdened by experiences and non-experiences. By the way, this is an experience that Nobody can have.

"The truth is called truth, and non-truth is named non-truth. However, because it is beyond all distinctions, it is neither called truth nor non-truth."

—Ta-Mo

PANTA RHEI

This path—our life—is actually an incomprehensible, inexplicable, uninterpretable and ultimately unfathomable mystery. However, life can also be Being, awareness and bliss. This awareness and joy mean that you never have to struggle against the flow of life or be surprised by the path. You are capable of endlessly rejoicing, of being imbued with bliss.

Despite the fact that one cannot describe the Oneness, nevertheless it is still vibrant, powerful, pulsating, vigorous and all-pervading. It is the force enabling us not only to live physically and emotionally but in our spiritual dimension as well. We ARE this life!

The above description is nothing more than mere words. These may confuse more than they explain. Even worse, words serve to make distinctions, and are also not capable of affecting the all-encompassing Oneness. What you are looking for on this path is well-concealed.

It is well-concealed in the wanderer.

It is the unfathomable Existence that is evading your attempts to grasp it. It disappears when you look for it. However, once the questions have dissolved and once the person (ego) posing the questions has disappeared, Existence will be the wonderful awakening in your Being.

Now try to let go. Try to abide in the state of deeply felt serenity that you have entered into. You will have arrived once you feel your fulfillment. Once your You is no longer there, Existence reveals itself in all its glory, in all its blissful fulfillment.

The Tao does not actively work, yet lo and behold, the seeming miracle occurs: nothing remains undone!

The Taoists call it Tao, the Buddhists call it the Buddha-Nature, the Christians refer to the Eternal Light, and the mystics talk about the Cloud of Unknowing.[49] Buddha named it the not-self, and the Hindus speak of Brahman. In Zen we call it the "primal insight"—an insight into what existed "before father and mother were born."

If you manage to solve the mystery by focusing on the "primal face," you will have become all that a person can be.

Let go of seeking and grasp it at this moment. Find it in the "Isness."

It is that which is inherent in all things, that which pervades and animates them, that which makes everything into that which it Is. It is what it is—the "Suchness."

What would omnipotence be if it were not all-pervading? Everything is divine and godly. This divineness has nothing to do with the image some people have of the Creator. Some picture him as having a long white beard, a lone wolf who is separate from his Creation and observing it, in the way that the dancer is separate from the dance.

This dualistic view clouds the fact that there is always a dance when the dancer dances. Dancing is not possible without the dance and the dancer. The dancing "creator" is thus inseparable from Existence. As long as the dancer dances, there is a dance. There is nothing outside of the cosmic dance. If the dancer does not dance, the dance stops. Then there would be nothing, neither a dancer nor dancing nor a dance.

All this corresponds to Buddha's teaching of emptiness and fullness. You are capable of seeing it all around you. You are capable of seeing Existence "living," "grazing," "watering," "fielding," "clouding," "sunning" and hear Is as the wind "blowing." When you perceive It in this way, you will feel godly and divine. You will perceive your divine Self as being that which gets up in the morning, that which takes in itself and all appearances.

Let yourself be what you are—a human being. Let yourself find your way back to the primal, the original and the natural, to what extends between Heaven and Earth, to what expands and contracts in the pulsating of the heart, to what lies in breathing, and in your supposed birth and death.

Once you have beholden this dancing of Existence, your petty complaining about superfluous problems on the periphery will come to an end. All that will be left is bliss.

Once this happens, it is time to be silent, to simply "be." Take advantage of the opportunity to enjoy this fullness and your state of tranquility. Let yourself gently descend into the depths of your innermost Being. Remember to be courageous. Bravery is called for because you are heading towards emptiness—nothingness.

Losing ourselves in nothingness is the chance to find ourselves!

This story takes place in ancient Greece. It is about Aristotle, and the walk that this philosopher took by the sea. Whilst doing such, Aristotle saw his colleague Heraclitus repeatedly scooping seawater with a spoon and then pouring it into a small sand pit. Heraclitus kept on fetching water. His purpose was to "transport the entire sea to this sand hole." Aristotle's response was to laugh. He pointed out to Heraclitus that he would never manage to accomplish his goal. In response, Heraclitus said that Aristotle's attempt to stuff all the knowledge about and insights on Existence into his head was just as futile!

The parting words spoken by Heraclitus to Aristotle were his conclusion: "Panta rhei—everything flows," which now takes on a greater significance for us. Heraclitus had noticed that everything is constantly changing and in a state of eternal flux, and thus that only change is real and constant. Accepting the fact that "one cannot step in the same river twice"[50] (because the river is never the same at any two given moments) enables us to realize the uniqueness of each moment. "It" flows eternally, meaning it is without a beginning or end.

Let us courageously enter this river. Being one with the flow is being one with life itself.

ENTITIES

WE NOW COME to an impassable area, a place where, as was the case with Chuang Tzu,[51] we "cannot know whether the butterfly has slept and dreamed about being a person, or a person has slept and dreamed about being a butterfly." Is there really a distinction between being awake and dreaming? When answering this question, please remember one of Shakespeare's most famous lines: "We are such stuff as dreams are made of."[52]

Parables enable us to get an idea of what will unfold for us on the pathless path.

While traversing this inhospitable area, a little "controller" comes out of the forest and merrily accompanies us. Surely you have experienced such a strange creature. Perhaps you did not recognize it as such. After subsequently allowing the controller to accompany us for a while, we are quite amazed to discover that such a controller seems to resemble the others that we know. If you know one, you know them all.

In actual fact, the controller was originally a "wannabe." Thanks to its stubbornness, persistence and strong will, it became aware of its desire to want to be someone who makes decisions for others and determines what other people should want—and succeeded in transforming itself into precisely that. So the wannabe proudly climbed the social ladder from being a wannabe to a controller. Its constant state of activity enabled it to silently promote itself. And, more often than not, professional qualifications were not even necessary to be promoted.

The simple wannabes are relatively modest compared to controllers. Notwithstanding this, the ego took advantage of the opportunities offered by being one of the wannabes. This led to the ego becoming even larger, even more dominant than the wannabe was whilst still alone. This caused the wannabe to strive to have the power to make decisions for others. This was the birthplace of the congenial desire to dictate what people should want and how they should be. This desire manifests the potency of being a wannabe.

The wannabe becomes a controller in order to be able to make better use of others to fulfill his own wishes.

Our reason for writing about these entities in our family chronicles is to enable you to immediately and finally transcend your self-chosen pain and suffering. You realize that you do not always have to be in control. Nor should you always want to be in control.

Actually, these two types of creatures are fundamentally very pitiable. They find themselves continually being coerced by the seeming necessity to subjugate, patronize, dominate, coerce and tame their fellow human beings. If one has enough of a desire to decide things at some point, these egoistic processes not only torment others. These strange creatures also torment themselves.

Naturally, such a statement appears to be dangerous in a time in which these creatures are being generated in such huge numbers. They are manufactured at the lowest possible cost, and provide questionable results. The dedicated machinery is said to produce the most convenient, practical, successful, leadership-oriented, powerful, productive and success-oriented specimens possible. These people are designed to cope with all the tasks we face in the world.

Hasn't the world been trying to convince us of the wisdom of "bringing out the best in us" and of exploiting our potential so that we can endure and sustain ourselves? Haven't we been clearly and repeatedly told that one first has to "become" somebody before we are allowed to "be"? Isn't it simply unbelievable that we have accepted and internalized everything originating in the egocentric depths of "authorities?" Isn't it incredible that we have dirtied and contaminated the diaries of our lives with these "instructions for being unhappy"?

There is nothing in these instructions about the need to be envious of the controller and the wannabe for claiming to justify the demands we have imposed upon them, notwithstanding the knack of these deplorable creatures for influencing people. The manifold attempts they make to shape and forcefully bring up people, as well as to mold, mislead and entrap them into believing they can and should be ruled by others are ultimately doomed.

Some people aim to do the impossible, which is the desire to add to or take away from Existence. This is impossible because the Absolute is already whole, complete and eternal. Nothing is missing, and there is nothing superfluous or out of place in it. People who do not understand this will one day realize the impossibility of their desire to perfect what is already perfect (for example, when it comes to the question of how to treat the environment or tampering with the food supply). This attempt to perfect what is already perfect leads to desperation. Those who assume responsibility for making supposedly necessary changes in the Absolute and voluntarily delegate responsibility for doing so to others end up becoming stressed and burned out.

Upon encountering them on our way, we advise these beings to try something different, to try doing the opposite. It might lead them to the following truth. The great Masters have shown us how we can free ourselves from suffering. "Lord, Thy will be done!" This prayer implies that you will lose your life if you cling to being in control of it, and that you will find your life in humility.

In humility we realize that what we already are is much more than what we could have ever made of ourselves!

Accepting this is deeply unsettling and shocking to many people. Nevertheless, it is comforting as well to have been shaken up so much in such a healing manner. It may lead to our experiencing the grace arising from being able to simply experience "Shikantaza," which means to mindfully sit in awareness. Once we allow ourselves to delve into our centers, we will be able once again to find tranquility and serenity.

Letting go and allowing ourselves to be where we are is all that we can achieve. Understanding this requires you to see yourself as having "arrived" at home (despite the problems you think you have). You now have the serenity needed to no longer resist the powers of Existence.

There are no longer any notions in your mind of your being a separate "I." These notions have been replaced by your having unfolded in your wandering, merging body, mind and soul in the process, and walking into the Oneness, which is actually an inseparable wholeness. Once we are ego-less in our doing, there is no longer a dualism between the doer and the doing.

In this case, there is only the wandering! Simply wandering entails complete devotion and dedication. In turn, this requires having trust in Existence. Deep peace comprises the original spirit that lies beneath all appearances.

Your "becoming" is realizing what you are.

Should you resist your inherent nature, you will be well on your way towards emulating one of these strange creatures whom we met. Deep despair, hopelessness and powerlessness in the relative world are the results of not wanting what Is, of not admitting what you really are and of accepting temporary reality as the ultimate truth.

It is up to you to make a choice!

"When we talk about concepts, we mean chained and blocked thinking. In contrast, non-thinking or having no ideas is the free, unimpeded action of the spirit. This already comprises the path, which is the path to truth."
—Ta-Mo

DIOSCURI—TWIN STARS

Roshi was the lovingly-applied name of an old teacher and Zen Master who also taught in Austria. He once responded to a variety of problems that people brought to him by saying: "The disadvantage is the advantage and the advantage is the disadvantage." At that time, this statement did not seem to be much of a help at all to anyone.

An ancient story from the Orient illustrates what Roshi meant. There once was a son who did not properly lock the paddock in which his family kept their horses. An expensive stallion got out and ran away. The neighbors came to the father to comfort him and to commiserate about his loss. The only thing the father said was: "We shall see."

The stallion returned on the next day. He was accompanied by a herd of noble horses. The family was congratulated by their neighbors. The only words from the father's lips were: "We shall see." His son subsequently broke his leg while riding one of the horses, and the father's neighbors once again expressed their condolences. The father repeated: "We shall see."

Shortly afterwards, soldiers arrive to forcibly draft young men into fighting a hopeless war. But the son was spared thanks to his broken leg. The father stated once more: "We shall see." The story continues in the same vein. What this all means, and what Roshi meant: We frequently ride the roller coaster that life truly is, a roller coaster in which good news may turn out to be short-lived, and tragedy may open up new opportunities.

It is obvious to us how temperamental the ego is, how this gives rises to all sorts of disadvantages. The ego does benefit us in one key way: it causes the suffering and distress that prepares us to show humility. Humility is the way for grace to flow and overflow in and through us, and that is surely an advantage.

In this interplay of our consciousness, there is always something to do, but also so much to let go of. Seeing through the egocentric mechanisms and tricks eventually helps to shorten the path. In turn, this will be lengthened by the other detours that you take to partake of the "sins" you approve of. This is a very human trait.

Mindfulness can help you to understand the dynamism inherent in your ego. This drive makes it easy to inflate your ego—and difficult to let go of it! We are likely to prefer people who tell us to "make something of ourselves" (to nourish the ego) instead of those—such as the authors of this book—who tell us, "Dump your ego and be what you are!"

We tend to believe what people tell us about what we supposedly are and what we are not. That is why we cling to our self-image, how we limit ourselves, why we admire and worship both idols and graven images.

We foster dissatisfaction, greed and desire in ourselves. Notwithstanding this, our state of unawareness causes us to denounce the consequences of this perverted behavior in our own children and condemn it as being degenerate.

Giving up the ego actually means not really having to give up anything. It would seem that relinquishing our ego would be equivalent to letting go of everything that makes us special. In actual fact, there is no sense of loss, but rather, one of relief. Living a life without the domination of the ego appears to be so threatening that we fear giving up our very lives. As it turns out, the bottom line is that we are only giving up an illusion, a mirage.

We let go of something we really never had, and, in return, get truthfulness and authenticity. This is not fake news, but the real thing.

All of the famous seducers in world history rose to power by flattering and strengthening our egos. Take Adolf Hitler and his cronies: they made the Germans believe they were the chosen people. Such propagations of falsehoods propagated and exaggerated by maniacs, yet incredibly effective, are the easiest way to win the hearts and minds of people. The mechanisms of the ego made the rise of Nazism entirely explicable. The Nazis pandered to the ego's overriding desire to stand out. And this is just one of many examples in human history.

The values and desires of the ego exploited by such "leaders" to forge an army of followers include emphasizing what is special, talking about the "chosen few," the only race with the right to live and a "God that only blesses our weapons." We have developed an ego prepared to do anything to be distinct and gain "honor," including spreading suffering and horror and even killing others (often in God's name). This is pure degradation and degeneration. The ego is precisely what separates us from everything and everyone else.

We would prefer to forego eternal light than do without our self-assumed identity!

Sticking to your ego causes bliss, happiness, serenity and spiritual development to fall by the wayside. This clinging is furthered by pseudo-religions which preach the strengthening of the egocentric process. Today's pseudo-religions are embedded in such ego-driven proceedings as our consumer-oriented society and political involvement, the image and status symbols they promise to produce and the desire for esoteric enlightenment.

Peace comes from uplifting ourselves by renouncing these substitute gratifications. When this renunciation is done on a temporary basis by sojourning in a monastery and by living a life of asceticism, the outcome is often a return to normal lives featuring a greater will to be ego-centric and results-oriented. The bottom line is that spending time in a retreat can also turn into a spiritual ego trip. By way of contrast, if we continue to go down the path of suffering, we may come to realize how little all the goods and lures of the world matter if we forget the Self!

We often come across people who use the word "egoist" as a curse word. Such people are actually envious of those people. A more appropriate response would be to pity such egoists.

Once you have started down the pathless path, your task is to consider yourself as having "gotten there," having "gotten settled," having "arrived at the Source"—and at this very moment. Finding is difficult while you are seeking. Nevertheless, you will soon find out that you understand the wind more often, that you more easily recognize music, and that you can adeptly follow cabaret. You will soon see that fragrances "taste like green," that your thinking has become more serene, and that it no longer oppresses you. You will begin to allow yourself to let go and feel at ease. A further benefit: those who do not know where they are going but want to get there more quickly will no longer keep you constantly on the go.

It is highly rewarding to become empty, to recognize what is supposedly profound as shallow and superficial and vice-versa. You will recognize that what we assume to be permanent is actually short-lived. Conversely, the short-lived mayfly will experience itself—through traversing this path—to be long-lasting for itself. That which seems to be familiar to us turns out to be mysterious, and that which was previously mysterious turns out to be something we are intimately acquainted with. Emptiness reveals itself to be abundance, and abundance to be emptiness.

You notice your state of being filled and fulfilled at the very moment of emptying yourself of your ego and upon letting go of your attachments. What we are referring to is letting go of feeling and experiencing yourself, and of the need to fill yourself with "content."

The abundance of grace fills you when no desires contaminate the space in you.

When you find the one Source and realize that you are the Source, you are Tao, the Way itself. There is no separateness or distinction between you and the Tao. In other words, you are also the origin. You are no longer separated from the path. What is left is the Self.

This is the way to get rid of suffering. The ways to grasp this are to discover the similarities existing among the world's religions and to appreciate the thoughts of the great Masters. This will enable you to view matters from the perspective of the "Masters whose eyebrows are locked." You will realize that everything is One.

Do you want to experience this state? Do you feel the longing to finally feel connected to the flow of gold-colored, energetic substance? Once you realize that you have reunited with the vital, biological energy, you will be flooded with Chi, your right to live, your claim to Oneness.

Everything becomes clear once the Source is no longer clouded by and tarnished with your desires, wishes, hopes and expectations.

The Oneness is and has always been pure and clear, bright

and expansive. Until you perceive this, the Oneness will be hidden under the images and illusions cast by such impurities.

The difference is only that there is Nobody who makes distinctions.

TRANSFORMATION

We should move along this path without intent in the same way we practice yoga or Qi Gong. We are capable of abiding in harmony and awareness of Yin and Yang in the relative world, knowing that supposed opposites actually complement each other. We draw strength from our center. Energy and strength flow freely and unhindered when you practice without intent or desire. The consequence of this is a return to the center and thus to the state of serenity.

The person who practices, assiduously and persistently devoting himself to the task of practicing, will be masterly in their modesty.

What is your plan to illuminate your spirit and to find your Being? How do you want to find what seemed to be lost? Once embarked on this path, you will immediately perceive what defines you only at the moment when you give up seeking, when you focus on what you are, when you let go of everything that you are not.

What about the people who opt to sweep the garbage clouding their perception under the carpet? Who are the people that are unwilling to recognize the sick attempts and the perverted approaches that we have made and unnecessary things we have accumulated? They are the ones who, like ostriches, stick their heads in the sand, who stubbornly give credence to false insinuations. They are the ones who work to cultivate and augment their egos, even though this often causes them to suffer agony. This arises from their obstinately insisting on denying their true Being. Suffering has no bearing whatsoever on their inherent natures in the realm of the Absolute.

Realizing that all our inner garbage is unnecessary liberates us.

So, persevere in your practice of not practicing. While doing such, don't get distracted by worries. Don't brood. Make use of your power of imagination to vividly evince what you are. Practice incessantly. It is the only thing to do.

Regard yourself as having arrived even before you get to the point of discovering your ability to let go in a big way. Tap this source of fulfillment and experience—divinely blessed in each moment—to see what it's like to simply allow yourself to be.

Do not let the rubbish thrown mislead you or cause you to lose your mind. Do not worry about your mind at all. It is the instrument whose only intention is to make you believe it does all the work for you. Of course, you have already realized by now that the mind is unsuited for many activities. Its operations are limited to cataloging, storing and combining things. YOU are intuitive and creative; you are the creative spark itself!

You have now discovered a talent that will take you further. In contrast, your mind will imprison your creative genius. This will be the case as long as you work intellectually, as long as you frantically mull over things. This process paralyzes and cripples your creative, inner power. It only reveals itself once you remain quiet and serene, once you cease to think. This is where meditation comes in. Meditation frees you from distress and misery by helping you finally let go and sit in peace.

Each religion has developed its preferred approach to

meditation. For example, it is possible to meditate in a resting position or while moving around. There is one thing all of the various meditation techniques have in common: they achieve movement in a state of calmness and calmness in a state of movement. How can a sitting meditation be considered nothing more than a state of serenity and tranquility? After all, you breathe while you meditate, and your blood circulates. Chi flows freely through the meridians. Similarly, why shouldn't movement instill serenity and stillness, provided that we are centered in our Being? In other words, when the mind abides in stillness and when thinking has finally stopped, movement becomes deep serenity, and you open the door to the divine.

Even though we are speaking to you, it is important to be aware of the fact that when we practice our techniques, there is to be no speaking, and the mind is to be silent. To attain this state, focus on the movement of Chi within you.

Focus on the essentials. The essential thing is to be mindful.

Train your awareness. It will ensure that everything turns out well. Your movement will be grounded when you feel the touching of the ground by the soles of your feet and reflex zones. While this happens, imagine that you have roots and that they reach to the center of the Earth. Each time you lift your foot to take a step, the movement is simultaneously a turning within and a dwelling in the Oneness.

If you are searching for a Western explanation for this phenomenon, listen to Albert Einstein and realize that everything is relative. So persist and persevere. You will make progress. The bottom line is that everything is One. If everything flows, as Heraclitus says, then everything is simultaneously motionless, and the only unchangeable thing is change.

By way of an example, you are completely in the here-now when you practice the self-induced movements in Qi Gong and when these flow of their own accord. You will practice in a free, unburdened manner once you have understood what it means to not interfere, to let go and to allow everything to flow.

Going on this journey through life is "being here," and that is enough. Being in the here-now means washing all behavioral rules, obligations, moral standards, systems and concepts down the drain. Your mind's response to this may be "anarchy!" But this is not at all true. The resulting state is not anarchy, but, rather "mindfulness."

Everything is unintentional and natural in the Absolute, Eternal, One Being, and there is nothing good and evil.

Why do we need regulations and laws? The answer is that they exist in order to enable the players to play the games according to the agreed-upon rules. The key question is whether the players exist to fulfill the rules. The answer: of course they don't! We are responsible for governing ourselves. In fact, it is the Self that handles everything.

What has just happened? Before we know it, we are once again entrapped and enslaved by our minds! We have yet to mindfully travel down the pathless path. This realization gets more and more powerful. The proper response is to gratefully accept what manifests itself and what the path opens up for you. Be humble, because at the moment the only thing you need to do is accept what Is—unless you want to change it. Then change whatever you are capable of changing. However, we fail miserably at realizing this most of the time. This is because we have a passion for wanting to change things that we cannot change. As the famous prayer goes, "O God, grant me the serenity to accept the things I cannot change, the courage to change the things I can, and the wisdom to know the difference."[53]

Go down the path of aimless wandering if you want to free yourself of suffering.

In this way you will also be standing in grace!

The key question is: how should we best practice? The answer: we practice walking in a light-footed manner, balanced and at equilibrium. Another question: how should you lift your foot and put it down on the ground again?

The answer: always do it mindfully, feeling each muscle in the process, being in harmony with Existence itself! First comes the inner movement, but don't hold your breath!

Be aware of your Self.

MOVEMENT AND STILLNESS

Inner movement comes before outer movement. It is the movement that triggers mindfulness and the accompanying breathing in you. You can let yourself flow in mindfulness. Your basis is your breathing, which in turn leads to movement.

Mindfulness will bring a new type of quality to your life, and not only in your physical movements. Your spirit will be more aware and mindful of your emotions. Letting go and letting yourself be touched by your innermost sanctuary means humbly accepting what comes from you. It means doing without your dominant will interfering and self-importantly taking control, or impeding the natural flow of energy due to its concern about losing out on some expected benefit.

The divine spark which flows comes from you without any action on your part. If you entrust your Being to it, it will take you on the waves of the spirit.

There is nothing, absolutely nothing, outside of the one Spirit. It is an arrogant and forlorn hope to think you could do anything without the One Source, or even resist it.

All the fruits of life come from you, the Self.

If any movement on this path seems cumbersome, do it as long as necessary until it seems easy. Recognize the forces of your inner Being at work. Feel how it moves you. In turn, this will serve as the basis for the free flow of life energy, or what is often termed Chi or Prana. The activity you initiate or the one triggered by outside events is not the activity which allows you to live in the flow, gracefully and blessedly. The Chi which you do not cause does that. It stimulates you, flows outwards, and expresses itself in a wonderfully harmonious manner.

Everything else is artificial, is superimposed upon you, and is based upon an image you have of yourself. Thus it is only an expression of your imagination. It pays to discard these false ideas and mistaken notions. When they stop influencing your movements, the expression of your-Self and everything it triggers in life will be authentic.

Let us return to the naiveté and innocence of the child. Be happy with your intellectual growth, but keep a childlike and innocent disposition and spirit. Move as you used to move when you were a child and you will feel a lightness of Being. Unlimited energies will then flow from your inner center, causing you to live, love, laugh, dance and experience joy. You are now alert. You are now enjoying conscious blessedness and blissful awareness.

You are the Self and only the Self Is.

Hurrying is now a thing of the past. It consciously moves you, and does so without the confusion usual to your movement in the past. You probably never observe with which foot you get out of bed. Sometimes we laconically observe that we got out of bed "on the wrong foot." You did not know what you were doing, and were unaware of your breathing. Now that you are more mindful, you are increasingly aware of whether your right foot or left foot is touching the ground.

If you are in a hurry, you should still go slowly. There is no confusion when there is no rushing.

In a manifestation of his compassion, a Master revealed to us how simple it is to develop mindfulness—by always entering a room with your left foot first. Now this difficult task is yours. An old saying calls upon each of us to "think before you speak." In the same vein, your job is now to be aware of what you are doing at the moment when you put down your left foot upon entering the room.

A person who has "turned on" her or his awareness, in the same way she or he turns on the light, will be less likely to smoke one cigarette after the other, get drunk, take drugs or cause people to suffer. You will sense her or his greater awareness.

"Switch on the light!"

MINDFULNESS

REGARDLESS OF HOW you move your legs, begin with your left foot. The spirit has no left foot. Therefore, we advise you to ask yourself whether you are really present in the here-now before you set about doing something! Ask yourself if you are aware, if you really hear it when you call out to find yourself. Look within yourself and see what emerges.

In terms of myself, Genro, it is sufficient to ask myself, "Genro, are you here?" At the moment I ask myself whether or not I am here, I am aware of my Self. Then I know that Genro is here—in a unique and irretrievable moment of being simply mindful. Reconnecting to the Absolute is not a one-time event that you experience and that enables you to subsequently rest on your laurels. Rather, reconnecting needs to be continuously renewed on a moment-to-moment basis.

This moment is eternal, because the next one comes after this one.

To have all the time in the world means having time to live. At the very moment in the here-now in which we ask ourselves if we are here, we are not lost in thought. We are thus in the right mindset—we are fully in the here-now.

What happens to those people who are so often lost and absorbed in deep thought, far away from their own Selves that they do not even notice what is happening around them? Time and space have vanished for them, and they are no longer able to be mindful of what is needed at the moment. Take the example of a man driving over the railroad crossing, unaware of the approaching train! It is seemingly impossible not to see the train, because the eye sends a message to the brain that "the train is coming closer!" But nobody was there. Our victim, whose car was rammed by the train, was dealing with his problems instead of being in the here-now, preventing him from being here with all of his senses and from doing the right thing.

Reflecting and pondering about things means we follow up our thoughts with more thoughts. This keeps us moving us away from the here-now. As shown above, this can be downright dangerous in some situations. This shows you that meditation is not some aloof, transcendental mulling over things but a very practical and very vital awareness. It gives rise to a conscious Being who is alert to his environment.

What happens to our spiritual powers and possibilities if we do not use them, or abuse and misuse them for other purposes to continuously reflect on things? Have you ever written down your thoughts while sitting serenely, and thought that you were not thinking at all? What happens in our minds is pure chaos. Our thoughts are undisciplined, acting like leaping monkeys spontaneously and willfully jumping from one branch to the next. "Thinking is a wild monkey" said Zen Master Linji. In fact, thinking is a confusing mess!

People cling to the idea that continuous thinking preserves us from harm. This false belief causes devastating damage.

Do not believe that constant pondering and brooding solves problems. Many problems arise precisely from these processes of thought, because they often cause you to experience sleeplessness, anguish and sorrow, worries and psychosomatic disorders. A further problem is that your mind generates top-heavy, overly intellectualized ideas, sometimes causing you to make fatal decisions in the process.

If you realize this, are unhappy about how things are going, and are looking for a way out, try something different.

Let go of thinking, center your-Self and gather yourself together in your inner space.

Your center is physically located below your navel, and thus deep inside your abdomen. The Japanese call it "Hara," the epicenter of people, and the Chinese call it "Dan Tien" or "Dantian," which means the ocean of Chi, the energy center, our life energy. How could you not be aware of this center? Haven't you ever felt that your uncertainty, despair and conflicts were based in the very depths of your stomach? Haven't you ever felt "sick to your stomach" and had a sinking feeling? Here is precisely where life vigorously takes place.

Our task is to live life, laugh and decide more intuitively and instinctively. All this involves—quite literally—feeling and thinking with our gut. Disavowing the area "below the belt" means forgetting and renouncing this vibrant part of us.

We often try to compensate for this disavowal by using our heads as a substitute. The results of this false equilibrium are bent, top-heavy people, insecure and desperate as a result of the constant and incessant flow of thoughts flashing through their minds.

The three Dan Tiens include the Lower Dantian, the main energy storage area, the Middle Dantian at the heart and its emotions and the Upper Dantian, the third eye where your spiritual powers are located. These three centers pervade us, nourishing, complementing and mutually depending upon one another. Our Chi flows freely and unhindered when these energetic gates and meridians are open and in harmony with each other.

However, all this will come to naught without the workings of the heart, which is precisely in the middle—three chakras below and three energy centers above! Without the working of the heart, existence is only materialism and sexuality is only pornography. Power without the heart only leads to destruction. Communication without the heart ends up as idle talk. Spiritual development that excludes the heart is only baseless, rational and intellectual reflection.

You are what you are. You do not have a choice in this matter. It is not a question of giving up your intellect in favor of your intuition, or vice-versa. You are to live in harmony with your nature, so as to ensure a balance between these two forces. In turn, this comprises the basis for our grounding ourselves, for our spiritualizing our lives. This enables us to live life as a being fulfilling its full human potential. Through this we become whole and we realize that we are blessed—as is everything that is lived and lives it-Self.

Only the Self lives.

UNITY AND PEACE

WHEN WE SEEK the truth, there are always ways to intensify and accelerate things, based on the idea that we have the capability to go faster, climb higher, delve deeper and further, and continue expanding and making progress. The mind uses logic to play this game.

We often call this a form of escape and its results are the last word on the subject—the be-all and end-all.

To see what we mean, let's return to the method of going back to the roots and the source. What existed at the beginning? The world. And what existed before the world? The universe. What came before the universe? Creation. What existed beforehand? The Creator. The mind is satisfied with the fact that the Creator created. Notwithstanding the mind's satisfaction, there is still a longing welling up in us. It impels us to ask that one important, final question. What existed before the Creator? Where does the One go back to? You may never fully have inner peace without getting an answer to these questions.

What does it mean when the being that seeks is the object being sought for, but cannot find it?

For this reason, we advise you to try something different for a change. Instead of trying to figure things out, allow yourself to be confused, and intentionally foment doubt. Do it as long as necessary until you no longer know how to go on and see that only the One remains. You cannot logically solve this mystery, because the mind is not the instrument you need for such work.

You will realize how to approach this challenge when you stop for a moment and turn within, when you realize that this mystery is a koan given to you! Absorb this problem like a glowing sphere in order to learn how to spit or vomit it out. Once you get rid of it because of the pain it triggered, once you finally learn the trick inside of it, realization will finally burst out of you, and will happen without you even thinking about it. The solution is letting go and detaching yourself from everything.

The German Chan Master Wolfgang Kopp put things in a nutshell when he called his book *Free Yourself of Everything*. The everything that needs to be done is to let go, to discard, to unlearn and to free yourself of everything. Then all will be well. This will be because you have pacified the supposedly divided spirit in you.

You will subsequently experience a very deep, sublime and blissful peace. You will let go, settle down on your haunches, or simply sit on your backside. You will have arrived to precisely where you were in the first place.

It is all there. Can you see it? If we could give you a whack, you might have the opportunity to wake up from your deep sleep. Of course you need grace. The question arises: "Is it only the chosen few, the blessed ones that receive grace? Why is grace required for us to be fulfilled?" While you are asleep, while you want logical answers—to satisfy your ego—place your trust in the blow you will get. It will awaken you!

However, when you are enlightened, you no longer ask these questions.

The Masters have given us simple methods that help you learn how to temporarily put your mind at rest and to stop thinking. For example, observe the breaks between the thoughts whenever you are mindful. Let your mind stray from observing the thoughts, and be mindful of the breaks. They are messengers bringing comfort and the way for the mind to become calm and to be the non-mind. You will experience with great joy that these breaks or gaps in your thinking get longer and longer. You will become increasingly clear in your awareness of being part of the One Mind that cannot be conceived or imagined.

You sat quietly before you first knew how to run. Your mind was quiet before your thoughts began.

It was possible to simply abide in tranquility prior to the commencement of concerns and worries! Where are you when you are in a state of deep sleep? How is it possible to be without awareness when you sleep, yet know about Being when you wake up?

You will become increasingly empty after wandering for a while. You may find it disorienting to move ahead in a state of "not walking," or to realize that when you take a break you are actually on the go. But it is this wandering, straying and meandering (as it seems to people who have not yet discovered this type of moving about) that will calm your searching, pondering, brooding and inquisitive mind.

Be quiet and mindful without thought. All suffering is alleviated and assuaged in this silence.

At first, tranquility may appear to you to be thoughtlessness or "thought-less." It may bear all the negative connotations of being carefree or inconsiderate. However, being without thoughts means not to think about and be concerned about everything. "Thoughtlessness" loses its aftertaste of being an unsatisfactory and inadequate mental state. Instead, it becomes something positive that we look forward to. Being without thought creates space for us to have healthy reactions and enjoy the instinctive, life-preserving impetus emanating from the subconscious.

A person will always find "reasons" to be unhappy, complain, criticize others, feel unfairly treated, explain why spiritual seeking is so difficult, and relate what obstacles prevent him from being diligent in his spiritual practice. One Zen Master had a simple, single response to every one of these reasons, to every possible excuse, justification or rationale. He would say, "Drop it!" Simply let go of all the thoughts, concepts and inner barriers you put up.

> **"The path is not something we can conceive of with our minds, so why should the path be dependent on thinking?"**
>
> —Ta-Mo

WU-NIAN

Enter the world of meditation if you want to practice Wu-Nian, or non-thinking. This will enable you to return to your center. This means withdrawing from your mind and ego-dominated existence, and delving deep in your breathing, body and feelings. Thanks to this, you will experience a state of deep serenity above and beyond all words, terms and synonyms, a state without the necessity to recommence thinking. You will transcend all substitute actions that we take to catalogue, standardize and typify reality in order to produce the concepts and images that we carry around with us.

Abiding in the state of "no thoughts" does not entail being unconscious, unaware and helpless! On the contrary, it means that you are in a state of being much more aware and mindful.

Conscious Being means being all-here—means seeing the reality coming in and out through the doors of your face, means smelling, tasting, hearing and feeling, means using your mind and observing how it works.

The mind usually engages in thought after it has "produced" something. For a conscious person, being without thought is a state offering a new and fresh quality to life, one that expands awareness. Without thought, you are completely in the here-now, and you can do things spontaneously.

You may wonder how a person can abide in "timeless Suchness." The answer is that all of our senses tell us how to abide completely in the here-now. After all, you are not capable of being anywhere else, of being in a different moment of time than now. We are thus always in this moment (even if our mind wanders) and completely here. You can experience the blessings of serenity on this journey along the pathless path. You do such by abiding in the emptiness of mind. The comforting thing is that this moment is eternal. It is followed by the next eternal moment and so on.

Be not afraid but rejoice.

How can we tell you in words what awaits you when words leave you in peace? How can we explain what it means when words are temporarily gone, when this takes you above and beyond non-differentiating wisdom, when this transcends thought and non-thought? There is no way to express in words how wordlessness tastes, feels, sounds—what it will be for you. Be courageous. You will grasp all this as soon as you stop thinking.

In the state of Wu-Nian, the absence of "non-thinking" is present.

In Wu-Nian, everything comprises Oneness, the big picture. All reality, which we previously referred to as the "10,000 things," is suddenly inseparable. You will not find yourself to be just a "part" of the Oneness, but realize there is only the Oneness, and you within. You will realize that the whole is greater than the sum of its parts.[54] You will see that the concepts you had about life kept you apart from life. Upon realizing this, a deep peace will abide in you, and you will be more alive than ever before.

GRACE

WE ARE ON a journey in the world of grace, which is granted unconditionally, whenever and wherever. It enables recognition and Self-realization. It is neither contingent upon anything nor is it something we can expect or count on.

Our seeking will be in vain should we strive to escape from the disciplinary actions of our mind by trying out everything available on the marketplace for esoteric products—and do such without regularly practicing and letting ourselves learn and unlearn.

The Masters speak about "collecting axes." What this means is that people collect all kinds of "spiritual" tools in their lives by taking many courses and trying out various methods, and do such without applying them consistently or long enough. This causes such people to have lots of experiences—but not the ultimate one. It is as if woodcutters collected axes but refused to chop down trees with them. In our case, our challenge is to chop down the "tree of knowledge of good and evil"—the tree of duality or separateness. Although we have so many tools at our disposal, the tree remains standing. We have to vigorously and persistently chop at this tree—without there being a woodcutter present. It is the absolute necessity of doing by non-doing.

Meditation is the purest form of non-doing.

The principle here is called Wu Wei. Abide in non-doing. Non-doing does not equal "doing nothing," because doing nothing is doing something. Non-doing means non-action, "effortless doing" and waiting for grace, although Nobody is waiting. Ultimately the goal is to "be"—which is beyond all doing and non-doing.

For this purpose, it is necessary that you observe all your drives, desires, preferences, wishes, hopes, expectations, fears, worries and all the other emotional processes that take place in your inner being over a long period. Of course, this will be difficult to do at the beginning.

It may seem unbearable to you to sit down and observe what is happening in you and with you, and to observe what is taking place in your feelings, mind and body. You may wish to stop and to devote your attention to the distractions enabling your ego to easily survive, but they distract you from your real Self. The ensuing struggle is between the ego and your observing mind, which is capable of recognizing the ego's processes and of putting an end to them.

It is only human that we try to hide things, to sweep all the junk and garbage that has accumulated in our lives under the carpet. Everything that succeeds in eliminating and dispersing all the rubbish is welcome. Just think, for example, of the opportunity constituted by watching TV and enjoying so much entertainment, sports and games. All these performances, activities and stress divert us from the need to look to our Self.

If all this is not enough to distract us, there is still the opportunity for us to escape into musing and brooding, enjoyments, addictions and illnesses.

The mind does somersaults and wants to prevent you from turning within.

It has every reason to do so and to play this game with you, because it fears that you will simply shut it down like a production line which is no longer needed. The mind is not interested in leading you to go above and beyond yourself. Neither does it have the tools to do so. It proposes all kinds of methods to make you think even more deeply, solve crossword puzzles and continuously train yourself "mentally." It wants you to get involved in complicated discussions in which you end up quarreling, thinking about and focusing on trivialities.

The most difficult demand of every true meditation is to neither form concepts nor to think about them. Meditation in Zen and other paths is designed to calm down your mind. It involves sitting on your backside, keeping your spine straight and counting your breaths. It gives your mind something to latch on to as a precautionary measure. This will forestall your mind's not being completely empty and your freaking out. In this case, the mind is similar to a grain mill which requires a few grains to operate so that it does not overheat.[55]

You will discover what serenity and equanimity are when you sit immersed and absorbed. You will not do anything at all except observe the gaps between your thoughts. After practicing for a while, you will ultimately be at ease. You will finally let go, no matter where you are, no matter how you are meditating, be it sitting in your chair or on your seat cushion. You will be without thought and in the present moment in which you abide.

You will have let go of your ego. Or rather, one should say: you have let go. Period. You have understood that always repeating the tried and tested patterns of behavior and playing the game of life in the same way you have played it since your childhood do not help you. You have understood that you have lived in an overly intellectual manner featuring an over-reliance on your mind. Subsequently you will also realize that meditation does not get you anywhere. There is Nobody to bring something to because there is Nobody who needs anything.

It is reality which affects us. It is what it really Is without the lies told by judgmental thoughts, ones that victimize us and our perceptions.

Call it whatever you want. What occurs is the "Isness." Non-thinking made this possible.

You will be receptive to the Divine when you have finally emptied yourself of all the conditioning bequeathed to you from your upbringing and from all the "moral training" that you received. This will dissolve the bondage and constraints within you! All this does not entail receiving something from the outside that you are now lacking, but, rather, finding it within you. There is no more seeking, only blissful discovery.

Nothing that your mind instructs you all of the time to fear is real. Remember what it may threaten you with in case you decide to meditate—to convince you that sitting absorbed and immersed in your Self, which is the essence of healing meditation, could ultimately lead to apathy, detachment and even alienation. Or that it is a waste of time considering your busy schedule, and only for a small group of "mystics". Or that you are not in the right "frame of mind" to do so or just isn't the right path for you. None of this is true! Wake up!

You will sense that the emptiness, the peace and serenity that you now feel and embody represent a new beginning. You will be in complete harmony between resting and movement. You will be able to abide in a state of well-being that you never imagined to be possible. This is because the body, mind and soul are in harmony with each other.

You ARE this harmony!

BLESSED ARE THE POOR IN SPIRIT

SEEKING OUTSIDE OURSELVES precludes finding what truly lies inside. The reason why we were not able to find what was seemingly hidden—the quintessential in us—was because we kept on running after things from the outside that had manifested in us. The virtually unlimited activities that we undertook in the real world meant that the Absolute was short-changed in our lives. Did we lapse from truth forever due to this? Was this our original sin?

We have the capability to use our intelligence to generate knowledge and to accomplish other things with our minds. If we fail to consider the key maxim of Socrates ("All I know is that I know nothing") and focus our attention exclusively on the knowledge we gain, we are in danger of losing sight of the mystery of life and Existence. The secret is in us, buried under knowledge. This means that you need to un-learn—in the full sense of the word—so much! Leave your mind behind and delve into the deepest secrets of life. Every night in deep sleep you descend to the source of your vitality and life force. In meditation, you discover—fully consciously—that you cannot recognize, describe or grasp the Source, the essence and the origin of your being. The Oneness, the Source—is not a thing or object that you can detect, perceive, take over or capture. Meditation enables you to find your "Original Face."

Returning to the source and origin of everything is absolutely necessary.

You have realized that you are not separated and alienated from Existence. Instead, you are a part of it, completely unconditional. You now grasp the fact that "I AM the only enlightened one under the sun," as Buddha said. Nothing in Existence is apart and outside of you and your all-encompassing Being.

This Being has the "I AM" as its eye and cannot see itself.

In other words, you are to flow with the calm and tranquil river of life energy, and to BE this river, and to BE the tall bamboo which, while existing in the flow of vital energy pulsating within you and enshrouding you on the outside, is accompanied and driven by this energy.

Accordingly, you will always find yourself in the infinite ocean of "I AM." There is no lack and nothing is missing. Your happiness is not dependent on outside events, on the fulfillment of desires or on success. You enjoy what life has to offer, and do so without being attached to it. You do not resist the flow of life, nor do you pretend that everything is peachy. There is an inner acceptance of what Is without being intoxicated with joy, and without letting anguish and despair drag you down into the pits. We embrace what Is even if our minds do not approve of what is going on in the world or in our lives. We do not want things to be different. Your eyes are full of love and compassion for all sentient beings. As an old Zen saying goes, "Every day is a good day."[56]

All desires disappear as you move along the path. This is in accordance with the principle of Wu Wei, doing by non-doing. As explained before, Wu Wei is not doing nothing, but is non-doing.

Realities come and go, and they fulfill themselves in their own ways. You do not resist this flow, nor do you strive to influence things, unlike your previous behavior, which was to attempt to shape the phenomena of life in accord with the concepts and ideas of your ego, which once believed in its separateness from reality. You are now at rest. You abide in the Oneness. Instead of feeling burdensome, this abiding is wonderfully relaxing, healing, light and pleasant!

When you flow with the river of life energy in your innermost being, everything is harmonious. Panta rhei = everything flows.

When you flow in harmony with the river, Consciousness is aware of what things are "right" for you and when the "right" time is.

When you do not fight against or resist the flow, your inner life is pleasant and cozy. You are gently carried by the ocean from which everything arises. You are aware of the Oneness. You abide in harmony as pure perception that is unable to perceive itself. This comprises the paradox of the subject.

Isn't it simply wonderful to realize that the only certainty we have is uncertainty? Emptying your mind makes room for the Divine.

When the door is open, you can go out into the open.

Who would not go through open gates if they saw them? Who would not escape into a state of freedom that liberates us from dependence on wanting and wishing? You will not know freedom until you experience the transcending of all preconditions and prerequisites. This is precisely the longing you have in your heart. It comprises the inner potential of your being. This will be fulfilled once you throw your fears overboard. These fears pretended to be protecting you from being harmed. In reality, they only stopped you from getting a taste of freedom! Without these fears, you get to experience real freedom, the real mojo. It is taste-less. It is free of any taste (or aftertaste).

Jesus expressed this truth in simple words in his Sermon on the Mount[57]. They show us that any form of mental acrobatics will ultimately lead us in the wrong direction. Jesus said: "Don't worry—live!" That seems to be a good summary as to how to get to the heart of the matter in a very up-to-date way. "Blessed are the poor in spirit"[58] is praise bestowed by Jesus upon those who are not constantly lost in thought, or tormented by reason or imprisoned by terms and concepts. Blessed are those who do not miss life by spending their time thinking about it.

They are the ones who are blessed and fortunate!

The mind is not the instrument we need to cause wisdom to blossom. Logic lacks the ability to take us where we need to go. As mentioned before, Albert Einstein's theory put things in a nutshell for all of us in the Western world: "Everything is relative!"

The all-encompassing Being is complete divine chaos.

Sometimes things seem to be a certain way, and sometimes they are, in fact, different than they appear to be. One cannot pin everything down, define, specify, deduce, calculate in advance, determine or want everything. Being encompasses relative logic, but logic cannot encompass Being.

It is the way it is! Every unique "Isness" is simply wonderful.

WISDOM

Y OU WILL HAVE become wise when you really feel in your innermost self that you are "in the world but not of the world,"⁵⁹ when you realize that thinking does not produce answers, when you accept that tormenting questions are to be resolved without resorting to thought.

All existential questions are resolved in the serenity arising from centering on the nitty-gritty, the bottom-line, the quintessential and primeval, and by focusing on your absolute Being and by giving up the desire to understand.

Sit down calmly, count your breath and observe the incoming and outgoing air in your nostrils. Although you have not received an answer, you are precisely at that place in the universe where you must be. You are capable of saying, "I AM THAT I AM."

Everything is happening at just the right time. You are free of your ego, which dropped away like an unwanted burden at the moment you stopped waiting for answers. The disappearance of the question and abiding in a state of harmony causes you to no longer need any kind of knowledge or realization.

Who would have needed it—and for what?

In other words, you are to call out your ego. You are to be flexible enough to evade its every attack. Be transparent. This will enable you to recognize the shady tricks of your mind, which poses questions you feel you have to deal with, and provides you with the "right" arguments for everyone and everything. Listen to what is said by a variety of people about a single issue. Observe how people dismiss, ridicule, minimize, judge, condemn or trivialize something. People like to glamorize, exaggerate matters. They love to cast their ideas as being the only viable solution or an inevitable logical consequence.

If you persist in thinking in a linear, inflexible and stubborn manner, you will return to inexorably moving in the wrong direction. You will be taking the cognitive path defined by the ego, focusing on proving your assumptions. This approach will lead you away from reality and the pathless path. It will imprison you in your self-made "castles in the air."

This detour is full of suffering. However, the bottom line is that it does not matter, nor does it change anything about the fundamental blessings of Existence.

Our agile, alert and flexible spirit enables us to escape from the steep cliffs of wanting, desiring, worrying, pondering, continually "taking care" of things, and incessantly focusing on doing. Our spirit helps us avoid dead-end streets and blind alleyways, and is capable of flowing in harmony with the ever-changing events in our material world and of being One with the infinite Tao.

The example of the bumblebee shows us the situation in which people persist as a result of their intelligence. The bumblebee is unaware of the discrepancy between its wing span and body weight. According to the rule of aerodynamics, this discrepancy means that the bumblebee should not be capable of flight. It still manages to do so.

People who "know" so much ultimately find themselves at a dead end. The professor specializing in the laws of physics finds it difficult to drive a nail into the wall. The doctor familiar with all diseases does not understand much about health. Knowing the number of muscles we move when laughing does not necessarily allow us to laugh freely. Having learned about love does not turn us into compassionate Buddhas, as war and mankind's cruelty and inhumanity show.

Everything we learn about religion and the knowledge intellectually catalogued in our brains ends up creating countless theorists characterized by their clever use of language. For the most part, such people are not able to reconnect to their original nature. In any case, this is something that each person can only experience himself. If people realize this, they will not spend any more time trying to interpret "sacred" texts, but will focus on standing firmly in truth and reaching the hearts of people.

Such a person will radiate love and compassion without attempting to prove the correctness of her or his teachings and methods that are designed to make people happy. This person will not try to use verbal or even physical violence to separate and distinguish herself or himself, but will instead recognize the interconnectedness of all and everything, as well as the Oneness which unifies people.

Recognize the light that shines in each of us upon deep tranquility's occurrence in the vast expenses of Oneness. You are now in the total presence of the Divine. Nothing in you asks whether or not this is the real thing! Questions no longer arise, and you look at truth with eyes that have been transformed, eyes that are radiating light. This is enlightenment!

Although the big things are simple, we are unable to grasp them!

Please take the time to consider the truly great people who have walked on the face of the Earth. They have returned to their natural state. The way they express themselves is just as modest and unassuming as it is simple. They show us the bare essentials, the essence of what we need, rather than sending us down complicated paths.

They complement the known with the unknown. Unfortunately that which is known entices us to neglect the unknown; that which is visible leads us to doubt the invisible; that which can be named makes it seem as if the un-nameable were untrue.

A wise person is unconcerned about both sides of these seeming dichotomies. He or she sees form but is aware of emptiness; he or she sees light but knows that it shines in the darkness; he or she knows one could not exist without the other, and that we are the only ones who separate truth into discrete phenomena.

Time is comprehensible only within the context of timelessness, existence in non-existence, and the dance of life is only apprehensible when there is no dancer who dances.

Life is recognized through death.

Opposites complement each other. Each set of these is derived from the One. But where does the "One" go back to? This is the mystery of life.

Accepting that this mystery cannot be solved is solving the unsolvable.

"When there is a concept, there is already thinking. Thinking contradicts the path of not having concepts. This is non-thinking, the path to embrace the truth."

—Ta-Mo

DOUBT

While wandering along the path, doubt may arise in you. It may make you feel disoriented. This should come as no surprise, in light of the fact that the path is pathless, the goal is indefinite, your companions are a bit "out of their minds," and you no longer know what you should actually do.

Let us foment doubt, realize uncertainty as the only certainty, and enjoy the complete absence of our presence.

The diffusive and mysterious nature of all appearances arising to the right and left of the path generate quite enough confusion. If you are capable of doing such, trust the natural flow of Being. This will ensure that you do not have to go anywhere anymore. Walking, involving simply putting one foot in front of the next, allows the path to arise. It makes you aware that you are simultaneously the activity of walking, the one walking and the way gone so far. You are the Suchness, which simply is.

"I AM the way, the truth and the life," says Jesus of Nazareth, pointing the way for us. He is a guide we happen to be encountering at this moment—thanks to grace. But remember one thing:

Don't consider the guide to be the goal!

Encountering, listening to and believing in a guide and other kinds of great sages are definitely awe-inspiring and helpful confrontations with awareness, Existence and the Self. But that's all they are!

All the pseudo-saints trying to convince us that the ultimate truth consists of recognizing the guides along the path as the ultimate goal only prevent people from fulfilling their mission in life. These people operate in professional disguises, as priests, scientists, politicians, life teachers and so on. Many seekers fall prey to their insidiousness or ignorance and stop seeking. These "professionals" stop seeking the Self, and stop us from doing so as well.

Mature and responsible mortals on Earth will find their way. They know how to use their minds as well as their intuitive mental powers. They enjoy the grace of having a longing for truth in their hearts. They feel the urge to foment doubt and turn within to their innermost core in order to abide and relax in Being, in the here-now. They will be whole, and like a phoenix rising from the ashes, will leave behind all the burdens of outdated and outmoded structures and "simply be as they are."

There are as many possibilities to reconnect to your own being as there are beings on our planet. But is this necessary if everything is encompassed within the Oneness? Everything is joined together in undivided, indescribable and inexpressible truth.

No human perspective or view of things is exactly the same as another. But everyone can arrive at the same insights.

The question arises: how can we believe it is possible to use a tool with inherent limits—our minds—to discover what is boundless and unlimited? How can we believe it is easier for us, who are supposedly on the highest rung of the evolutionary ladder, to allow ourselves to simply be beneficiaries of Existence? How can we believe that it is more pleasant not to accept the sobering fact that Existence does not bother with the games played by our egos, and does not care about our knowing or not-knowing?

How can we engage in discussions about things of peripheral importance and how can we keep our eyes trained on outward appearances and still hope to discover the infinite, the cosmic and deepest secrets? How do we intend to find what is concealed deep inside by looking on the outside, and by continuing to postpone our turning within and returning to the Source?

Continue having grave doubts. These will keep you alive and in the present! Do not let yourself be confused by bewildered people who, in a worst-case scenario, intentionally misuse and deceive you for their own purposes. For instance, we encounter such deceivers as the capitalistic propaganda of materialism. It systematically exploits our egos to get us to become slaves to mammon—to material possessions and wealth.[60] Communism, seemingly the absolute contrast to capitalism, has also been known to employ deceit to gain control over people's thinking.

As an ego you are beneficial because you dream of benefits.

Does this sound like you? Once you accept the truth about yourself, you will know it about everyone else! We are all One in the Oneness. Everyone has the Buddha Nature. Once you are aware of this, you will encourage and support people—by providing love and compassion—as they wander along the path. You will share with them what you have learned so they do not have to repeat these bitter experiences, so that they will not reinvent the wheel. By way of contrast, should you act egoistically, you will rob others of their false hopes and disappoint them again and again.

You will fight against those who intentionally bear false witness, just as Jesus drove out the money sellers plying their trade in the temple.[61] Were Jesus alive today, he would not shrink from doing the same thing again, and he would probably suffer the same fate for it.

It is a rule that we as human beings tend to crucify those who out of compassion beat up on our egos.

Let us consider Socrates and Osho, who were poisoned. Let us bring to mind Pythagoras and Martin Luther King. They and other beloved wise men and women became victims of fanaticism. The fanatic ego does not want to be left alone. It considers not being able to simply be a beneficiary as an appalling and outrageous injustice.

The ego regards non-thinking, being humble and putting aside our incessant wishes as being unpopular and seemingly destructive forms of behavior. The ego's practices have facilitated the rise of Hitler, Napoleon, Stalin and others. There is only one correct response to a false leader striving to persuade us that our race, skin color, religion or whatever is "the only right one," so help us God!

A case-in-point is the Third Reich, which used deceptive and dubious cleverness to get the masses to view themselves as the "chosen people." Look at what happens to human beings that are misled by their egos, when they insist on believing in duality, and when they refuse to abide in Oneness. See the consequences of people paying homage to the lures of the relative world, instead of exploring their innermost sanctuaries, when they view others as strangers instead of as divine beings endowed with the Buddha Nature.

All these people are caught up in the supposed conflict between good and evil. Many even lust for power. Such people are capable of just about anything, including the most vicious and despicable deeds imaginable. Just about anything is possible in our relative world.

On the other hand, take a look at the enlightened way of life groups of people have led—such as the American Indians prior to the arrival of the Europeans. The lives of the Indians manifested the harmonious co-existence of their culture and nature. Their beliefs challenge today's ecological perspectives and practices. The lifestyles of the Indians were destroyed by arrogant and false interpretations and convictions, which today have brought us to the brink of an environmental disaster of unprecedented proportions.

The mind, our instrument of thinking, is occupied with playing its own mind games. The game of destroying the environment is now followed by the game of trying to save it, which we are doing halfheartedly. Higher ethical and spiritual values of life are not accorded a priority by shortsighted decision makers. This is because these values do not generate any direct measurable monetary benefit. The game of destroying our health is followed by the game pursued by orthodox, Western medicine of restoring it. We are moving around in circles. First there is destruction followed by restoration, or construction and then smashing things apart. Shiva is laughing.[62]

Observe human history. It repeatedly shows how seemingly powerful cultures got fat and lazy, and were forced, at the pinnacle of their success and of their decadence, to plummet to their starting points. This pattern arises because the natural gets largely lost in a self-destructive frenzy.

You may well continue using your mind to solve the problems in the relative world. You may well continue to let your mind "expand" with knowledge, experience, routine, new methods etc. You may well allow your mind to continue to play dualistic games—so far so good!

However, you will have to abandon your reliance on thinking in journeying within, in searching for the Absolute and the ultimate, deepest truths. Or you can delve deep, and you can feel what you need to find your innermost center, inner space and the source of your biological energy. Ask yourself where this energy comes from.

Don't let yourself be distracted by views and lookouts on the pathless path. Consciously and mindfully find your way to the Self, which is under the soles of your feet.

Walk deeply and mindfully in every step, every movement, and nothing will stand in your way.

Above all, you yourself will no longer stand in the way of your Self!

Become increasingly aware of the fact that in wandering you are familiarizing yourself with the path.

The blindness, delusion and confused state of being which held us imprisoned and which was the result of the garbage and filth we collected immediately clears up once we no longer see life and its challenges and tasks as obstacles, ones causing conflict and unsolvable problems. We simply start realizing how wonderfully simple Existence is.

It begins with the lilies on the field and the birds which put aside small quantities of food for the winter, culminating with people endowed with the gift of consciousness.

All creatures learn to live in the awareness of their existence.

Everything unfolds in harmony once you refuse to superimpose morality and immorality on your thinking, once you learn to flow with the river of life. It teaches you to pleasantly relax. You are no longer exhausted and dejected by the blows life throws at you.

Instead, you are uplifted and vigorous. Your energy is not going to separate big from small or good from evil. You no longer engage in making distinctions. Rather, you abide in your inner space. The moralist and his judgments are not capable of tempting or luring you away from your inner serenity. You are no longer hassled or harassed about how you think. You now rely on the intuition issuing from your innermost Being, which spontaneously guides you. As the famous Zen Buddhist monk Thich Nhat Hanh reminds us in his books, you are now capable of seeing each person as the Buddha and every object as a reflection of the Oneness.[63]

You are awakened. You move in wakefulness among sleepwalkers. You guide those accompanying you on the pathless path. You refuse to allow the mechanisms and machinations of "society" to prevent you from claiming your right to Oneness with the Absolute. You live in the awareness of your Original Being. You are always conscious of the fact that it cannot know itself. Existence is not a thing that can be known or controlled.

The true mission and destiny that we have the right to claim is to be in a pulsating interaction and interrelationship with all sentient beings. You feel the divine spark at every moment, the spark radiating from the inexhaustible, infinite depths of eternity.

Fulfilled Being means living the Self by experiencing and

embodying what and how we really are. Imbued with the Self, there is no longer anybody separate needing to be imbued. Only the Self remains. Realize the I AM THAT I AM during meditation, in silence and inner peace. Have faith!

When you can perceive the sound of "one hand clapping" or know "the taste of green," you will realize that you are free, and have actually been so from the very beginning. Perhaps you will have to continue along on the pathless path a bit longer; perhaps you will have to feel it a bit farther under the soles of your feet until you reach this point. However, where will you go if all this happens outside time and space, in a state of chaotic unpredictability?

We have to detach ourselves from the illusion that we have to know everything. We have to forgo our need to judge, describe, categorize or reject things. We have to renounce our belief that we have done enough simply because we now think we understand what is going on.

Pride and arrogance torment people satisfied in believing they have a sufficient knowledge of things. However, they are far from truly "comprehending" and fail to delve to the One Source.

It is a relief to exercise humility and participate in Existence. We embody the naiveté of the wondering child, one who shows a natural, unprejudiced and clear consciousness when confronting life, who sees itself as being undivided from the Oneness, and who graciously accepts Beingness as it is. This childlike naiveté embodies the amazed, inspired and innocent looks down the valley and up to the mountaintops. It neither compares nor focuses on differences and distinctions.

The child who looks at life with clear but dreamy eyes has both feet firmly planted in the ground, is close to reality, and refuses to consider Existence as a mere object. "Becoming like little children" means to live completely without intention, in innocence and by grace. It enables initiation into the ultimate mysteries of life. Doing so may involve simply standing enraptured in front of a work of art or a work of nature, such as the web of a spider or the panorama of the sky.

A wise person has the eyes of a child, bowing his head before the wonders of Being.

The childlike nature is pure, innocent, completely whole and unspoiled by any arrogant categorizing of things. It does not differentiate, separate and divide. What could its spirit be bound to?

THE JOURNEY WITHIN

In wandering along the pathless path, do you see how you can understand things?

Accept the fact that you cannot know it.

You are now capable of abiding in a state of not understanding, because letting go is actually the great realization. What you used to consider as understanding actually only consisted of illusions, presumptions, vanities, prejudices and concepts.

To go down the courageous path of intentionally doing without understanding means giving up the desire and need to understand. This path will lead you to self-lessness. By letting go of understanding or the desire to understand, you also let go of your ego.

You are already the Buddha, also when you sit in meditation.

Realizing this brings both bliss and the need to master the difficult challenge of overcoming the processes in our mind. It has been conditioned to want to know everything. It therefore finds itself in a state of ongoing restlessness until it finally is capable of making judgments.

Aren't we imprisoned most of the time in a state in which we strive to increase our so-called knowledge? The mind tries to fill every supposed gap in its knowledge with as many insights as possible, with more facts and sensory perceptions, not to mention all its worries, pondering, wanting and wishing. The mind does this until the limited "I" of the individual is blown up to be as big as a balloon. When your head is crammed and all the energy and strength in your stomach is diverted to play intellectual games and mind-numbing exercises, you will feel you are no longer in your right senses and no longer fully present.

When this happens, you will have gone astray. You will have allowed yourself to be tempted and to be confused by questions which torment you instead of letting go. No matter where you may be, realize that you are always whole, complete and eternal. You are always unconditional, one with the Oneness. Realize that if you do not let go, you will wander in profound blindness, unaware of the bliss that is yours to enjoy.

Meditation helps you see through the process of illusion, and to realize the game that your ego is playing with you. In meditation, all burdens selflessly fall from your shoulders. There is nothing you have to trust and need to strengthen yourself with because you already are what you seek. Your laugh rings out loudly, reflecting your joy in the unborn and eternal, in what always was and will always be. You can now experience this wonderful, indescribable joy. In laughing there is Nobody who laughs—only the liberating sounds of joy.

"It" is what was awake and present in you "before there was a father or mother," which is not born and does not die. It is that which is eternal, above and beyond the concept of mortality.

What you realize in yourself is immutable, unchangeable, does not age and is that which you immediately recognize again upon waking. Astonished, you realize that you are in deep sleep. It is hidden and yet so apparent:

You ARE <u>before</u> awareness ever existed!

When you let go in your Self-lessness to the extent that you even let go of wanting to know yourself, then you have finally arrived. You can say "I am neither the body nor the mind. I am not my emotions, thoughts and concepts. I am not my storyline, life history or supposed identity. I am neither the past nor my experiences. I am not the film being played out. There is no other place I need to be, nothing else I need to do and nothing I need to acquire, accomplish or attain. I am more than all these phenomena. I already AM. I AM the Oneness, the Suchness, the Isness."

However, you will never grasp this if your interests are sparked by the banalities of daily life and if you are fully occupied in your intense pursuit of things on the periphery of life. You may have an overflowing accumulation of possessions in which you store your harvest—the fruits of our material, relative world—but you will have not come any closer to the Self.

You yourself are the mystery, the longing in you which graciously has you seek and suffer until you take the journey within.

MEDI (as in meditation) means returning to your inner core, making yourself whole once again. When you empty your mind, you teach it to win by having it practice losing. It is about losing your ego and dispensing with objects on the outside, and letting go of the concepts and image you have of yourself. When it is only the observer who remains to witness what Is, you will be in a state of Self-realization in which you return from diversity to Oneness. You will find out that there was no beginning before thinking and thus no end after thinking. Your Being is eternity, the timeless "I AM THAT I AM."

This process is something one cannot describe or talk about, because it takes you above and beyond the limits of cognitive thinking. Remember that you have the capability to be one with the pathless path and thus to be the empty bamboo in the flow of your life energy. This bamboo is wide open at both ends.

You are flooded but also surrounded by energy, shrouded, protected and preserved in the flow. You do not differ from this flow and the Oneness.

As a result, there is an end to our man-made concepts of above and below, behind and in front of, warm and cold, right and wrong, holy and sinful. As a result, you experience what is real and authentic. You no longer make distinctions and are no longer separated and different from all of Existence in which you now flow. You stand in the Oneness, are All-One, and have awakened to the truth. You ARE this truth!

You are as open as the "vast expanses" which Bodhidharma reported about to his emperor. Encompassing the Allness, you also encompass all opposites. Everything you felt you had to distinguish or which kept you apart now goes with the flow. You no longer cling to what is transitory and illusive. The grace of letting go has freed you. The serenity and equanimity of being in the here-now leads you to your innermost harmony. You experience fulfilled longing, when all opposites are seen as having dissolved, and you no longer believe yourself to be on the outside.

It is actually so simple. This is because it has always been here. The laughing emanating from you arises from recognizing the harmony that was always yours to enjoy. You have transformed all doubt into a deep and all-encompassing trust.

Self-confidence is confidence in the Oneness, the existential state of Being underlying everything.

The Self no longer makes distinctions, is perfect in its imperfection, and encompasses everything—and thus naturally all opposites. Ramana Maharshi once said: "If you know the Self there will be no darkness, no ignorance, and no misery."[64] And Marcus Aurelius, the Roman emperor and philosopher, stated: "He who lives in harmony with himself lives in harmony with the universe."[65]

THE RIVER OF LIFE

No person's thinking—and no human imprint—influences the river of life!

On the pathless path it is necessary to completely empty yourself so that it can happen instantly. Empty yourself of all contents, especially what has been (im-)planted and imprinted in you and what you have been taught. You are involved in a process of unlearning and forgetting. It will lead you to experience an increasingly clear feeling for the infinitely vast expanses of space. Be open, serene and tranquil. There is nothing that you do not embody in these wide open spaces which you can perceive. There are no skeletons in the closet and dusty furniture as obstacles to the Divine.

When it takes place, you no longer have to ask and no longer will. The questions you had will have dissolved, and you will have arrived without having received the answers. The question of whether or not you have "reached" the goal is no longer an issue for you. You are not different, even in non-difference.

Enlightened beings never ever have doubts again, not even for a moment. Only the person who is asleep, by way of contrast, is imprisoned in his dreams. He spends his time wondering whether he is awakened or asleep. The awakened and enlightened one is like a guard, like a warrior who mindfully goes along the path after having trained his awareness. Now he wanders about with open eyes and an open heart. We are tied to ideals and visions as long as dreams lead us to believe in an unreal world. Our wishes, ideas, hopes and fears keep us in a world which torments and imprisons us. This trait is profoundly human but limits us.

The awareness of darkness and imprisonment corresponds to the symbol of hell. We voluntarily live in our self-made hopelessness. This is perhaps due to a lack of motivation or of perseverance to tirelessly struggle to be awakened, to be enlightened and to give grace a chance. We abide in a state of unawareness, and thus inflict immense suffering on ourselves and others.

We cannot yet see what Is and do not know what we are doing! The fact that you place your trust in someone who knows the path is a beginning. However, sooner or later, the true companion on the pathless path will point out to you the necessity for you to go alone. It is the opportunity for you to awaken.

If you want to awaken, you also have to wake up from the dream of irresponsibility and the need to be guided and take your life into your own hands.

Viewed in this light, all teachers, masters, leaders, guides, gurus and enlightened individuals are ultimately unnecessary. To be completely mindful for just one moment means seeing! And seeing means you have opened your eyes and no longer dream.

Once this happens, you can dance and sing with the

enlightened ones. You dance because the emptiness in you is filled with divine grace and because life flows from all the gates of your consciousness. This life no longer considers itself to be separate and detached. Instead, we realize ourselves to be originally inseparable from all that Is, from all Being.

> **The entire universe takes care of you because Existence is not separate from you. You cannot help but wander along the pathless path.**

You will experience a completely new spiritual state when one thing becomes clear to you. It was the human mind which was responsible for dissecting and denying the original Oneness of Being. The mind seized on the crazy idea of dependencies between the linked parts of an unnaturally complex setup.

In this undivided spirit, tranquility, serenity, calmness and peace have a healing effect in your innermost being, no matter how loud and compelling the external noises and distractions may be.

It is all so simple that it remains inexplicable to our brooding minds. How can your mind and its logic accept the fact that you harvest the abundance of grace, bliss and the full awareness of Being upon emptying yourself and your existing selflessly?

It could happen that people going through a similar development will display interest in your search, and, above all, in your "discovery." If you continue along the path and delve more deeply into the mysteries of Existence, you are likely to see things you never realized before and may find difficult to accept. Your insights into your everyday life, into relationships and into the world in which you live will change.

Your exploration of your Innermost Being is hardly perceptible to people on the outside. While you are on the path, the value of such a profound exploration may be called into doubt. This will be because you will have not yet reaped the fruits nor harvested them in the storage of your experiences. But how can other people who are asleep understand someone in the midst of awakening?

You will be temporarily alone in your attempts and exercises, in your process of reconnecting to your inner Being and in moving along the pathless path. Is there anyone you can bring to understand what you have gained with this clear view of things? Do you really think you can get someone rooted in entrenched, linear and dualistic patterns of human thinking to understand what you—we—are experiencing along this path?

You can stop when the path becomes the goal. When you are moving forward, you will have ample opportunities to stand still and sit down. You will be capable of living your life in peace and in a composed, serene manner, one free from desperately running after illusions and delusions.

But who will be able to understand you? Who will be able to believe that she or he could join you on the pathless path? Actually, you could accompany each other, take turns, and know there is sufficient room for both of you to the left and right of the path.

Is it important that thinking is complicated and one takes simple actions? Or should our actions be complex and our thinking simple? Are both correct approaches, or are they both misleading? The bottom line is that all great things are simple. However, this does not stop people from indulging in thinking in complicated patterns, in mulling over and reflecting on things afterwards. People are prone to boasting they have to deal with "difficult lines of thought." Abstruse ideas are frequently created. Mental acrobatics are performed. The results of these overly intellectualized reflections and actions are both actions and failures to act. These in turn cause great distress to all sentient beings.

The time and space in which you move along the pathless path are infinite and simultaneously here at this very moment. "It" is broad but sometimes so narrow that you cannot go through, like the eye of a needle. "It" is often so difficult that "It" cannot be grasped, and sometimes so easy that "It" may not interest you. You have once again reached something that you cannot explain. The path is mystical. Unsolvable mysteries arise from your attempts to solve them.

You can let go of thinking. And, by the way, don't let others think for you.

If you have traveled along the path in self-forgetfulness, then you have surely noticed that mysteries are revealed on their own accord. There is Nobody who could become the knower, possessor, owner or victor.

There is Nobody to become the enlightened or realizing one through Self-realization. The ray of light which the spiritual eye makes you see hits the divine in you—which has always known it. It only takes a bit of tranquility, emptiness and gracious serenity to reach what you have always been.

Only this time around, there isn't a Somebody who has arrived, and Nobody who can be said to have arrived. This is the only way it can happen. At this very moment, the Divine is embodied in the one who no longer identifies with the role models, who no longer sees things in himself as ideas and concepts. The Divine is embodied in this Nobody, in receptive emptiness, in vast open expanses and in immeasurable clear consciousness.

"People have something they want to achieve, instantly triggering illusion. The wise one does not want anything he still wishes to achieve, which is why he is free from illusion. Good and evil arise immediately from illusions. There are no distinctions without illusions and also no non-distinctions."

—Ta-Mo

VAST EXPANSES

What remains for us to do is to create the prerequisites enabling tranquility, peace and serenity to blossom in us. This will serve as the basis for enjoying the blessings of re-connecting—to our original Being, to the cosmic dance, to the Buddha Nature, to the all-encompassing soul or to the Divine. You can call it whatever you want: it is what you are!

Such an experience is like an unveiling or uncovering. It is as if you took away the blanket and found everything that was covered beforehand, but was always there. It was inconceivable and unimaginable, and will remain so.

While you slept, you were not aware of lying under the blanket. You were also not aware of being unaware.

When you get up and take away the blanket, you will see what you already had an inkling of. It is something that you would never have dreamed was possible, but that you were aware of before you fell asleep. It was something that was already there, which you were aware yet unaware of, with this depending on how deep your sleep is and upon the extent to which you wander in a state of inner wakefulness.[66] And now it is right in front of your spiritual eye. You no longer doubt. You no longer have to rely on faith.

As the great Indian poet and mystic Rabindranath Tagore[67] wrote: "Faith is the bird that feels the light when the dawn is still dark." But now the darkness has truly given way to light and bright. Knowing, seeing and realizing have replaced the vague ideas, worries and fears you once had. Teresa of Avila said, "Whoever has God lacks nothing. God alone suffices."[68]

"Where we are, God is, because there is no longer separation or division.... That which I am seeking, I am," said the American mystic and spiritual teacher Joel Goldsmith, adding that God-consciousness "is the all-power and ever-presence which will never leave you nor forsake you."[69] God awareness is Self-awareness.

The very first perception upon waking is to be taken as the irrefutable gift of God that you ARE and that during the previous night you were in a state of awareness and unawareness. Comprised in this gift is the realization that you were not aware of this unawareness while you were sleeping deeply!

You are free but you no longer linger in this realization. You let that go as well because it has become meaningless. Who is interested in his condition when he is completely whole and holy, when he moves ahead in complete inner health and wholeness? Who is interested in his status or reputation when he confronts all sentient beings with a loving heart, and knows in his innermost being that he is connected and one with the All-One?

In the awareness of the all-encompassing Oneness, one gets a hint of the Source of Being, which remains unrecognizable, unknowable and mysterious.

You proceed without abiding. You give and take and infinitely love without attachments. This is a state without a beginning and an end, because it is only Being—conscious Beingness and bliss!

While we linger at this place on the path, we would like to tell you the story of a compassionate Master in India who repeatedly tried to give his pupils a better understanding of truth. To this end, he gave them images, parables and stories. One of the latter is below. Nobody knows whether the Master invented it or reconstructed it from older sources. It really does not matter, because the story is wonderful in any case, and because it gives us a deeper insight into the relationship of a Master and his pupils.

Once there was a king who had a huge realm in today's India. The king strove to gain both knowledge and wisdom. For this reason, he was interested in all wise teachers and what they preached. The teacher who impressed the king the most was an old Master. The Master spent his time preaching and sitting serenely and calmly in meditation on a spot on the path between the village and the nearby palace. The Master subsisted on the rice and millet brought to him by his followers. People thought that the Master could help the king to become even richer, so he was invited to come to the palace. The Master gladly shared his wisdom with the king, but he also took part in all the dancing, games and other pleasures that the king and his entourage enjoyed.

After several months of the Master's living at the palace, a question naturally arose. It is the same one we usually think of when we see a Master who is deeply human. One day the king said to his teacher, "Excuse me, but I have to ask you something. What is the difference between us? You eat the same food as I do. You enjoy the same amusements, and are just as much a guest as anyone else. I can't see the difference any longer! How am I different from you or you from me? What makes you the Master; what makes me the pupil? What can I learn from you if you do the same things I, my family and all my friends do here?"

The Master said to the king that he could not give him the answer in the palace. The king was asked to follow him to the village road, where the king had seen him for the first time. So they continued walking along the road. The palace was not far from the border of the kingdom. So they soon reached it. The king said to the Master, "I cannot follow you any longer. I have reached the borders of my empire. Here I have all my riches, my family, my power and reputation. I cannot abandon my people. I cannot come with you."

The wise man laughed and replied, "Now you can see the difference! I wander and nothing holds me back. Nothing keeps me here, and there is nothing I have to let go of. I own nothing in particular. Therefore everything is mine! Not only your kingdom but all kingdoms are mine! My Being encompasses the vast expanses, which are infinite and eternal. That is the difference between the two of us."

Naturally, there really is no difference at all. The king simply thinks there is one. He doesn't need to undertake anything special. All he has to do is to simply let go of his self-imposed constraints. He has not reached the same point in his consciousness as the Master, but he has the same consciousness as the latter—as we all do. Remember the example of the small and the tall bamboo. The king will see himself as being inseparable from the Oneness once he has achieved enlightenment.

You will have begun to awaken when this difference becomes perceptible to you, when you can realize what or who in you is the attachment enchaining you and keeping you in bondage in the kingdom with its borders. This bondage has reduced you to a mere fraction of your potential. However, doubts as to your present course enable you to begin awakening to it. Doubt makes you attentive to and mindful of what you imagine and envision. Prior to doubting, you were prepared to sacrifice your freedom in the name of these concepts and images of yourself. They prevented you from blossoming like the lilies in the field and being like the birds taken care of by their heavenly father.

The story above has a similar message to those of the great Zen koans. One koan is about the young goose in the bottle which is fed until it is fully grown. The koan asks: how do you get the goose out without hurting it or breaking the bottle? That is the predicament.

Let's consider the response of Zen Master Joshu to the question of whether or not a dog has the Buddha Nature. His reply: "Mu." This means nothing or nothingness or "without." What is this supposed to mean?

What about the statements made by wise people throughout history? One of them was Seattle, the chief of the Indian tribe of the Suquamish Indians. In 1855, Seattle sent a letter to Franklin Pierce, who was president of the USA at the time. The letter asked Pierce, "How can you buy or sell the sky, the warmth of the land? We do not own the freshness of the air or the sparkle of the water. How can you therefore buy them from us?" This touching insight moves us. In it, we recognize the wisdom provided by a free spirit. This stands in stark contrast to the limited and limiting idea of self-marketing.

The ego is often not open to such teachings. That is why many continue to cling to possessions, knowledge, power, recognition, things and, sometimes, painful relationships.

We never stopped accumulating material goods. We never stop devoting energy to determining who is good or evil, right or wrong. We spend our time discussing who actually deserves property, power and recognition—naturally in accordance with our egocentric opinions.

The way for you to return to your center is for you to turn your back on outward appearances and return to your innermost Being. You will understand why you are doing such upon reaching this place of energy and strength! From a spiritual perspective, there is no individual "I," "my" or "mine." You will no longer separate yourself from others once you no longer egoistically pile up earthly treasures in the manner described above. Once you cease doing this, you will no longer be disconnected from the universe. You will be imbued with everything. You will be permeated with Oneness. It is a question of yielding to the powerful floods of Existence, and of accepting the risk that the old "you" will no longer exist.

You will no longer exist to make distinctions, to exclude, to alienate and to limit yourself to being on the periphery. You will no longer see yourself as an isolated island. Instead, you will exist as the ocean, as the universal force of Existence.

You can play with all these terms and concepts, because there is Nobody left to make distinctions. It is impossible to describe what is infinite, eternal, all-encompassing and nameless in words. The only thing we can do is use a parable like the great Indian saint Bodhidharma who brought Zen from India to China, "Vast expanses, nothing holy."

Everything said and written here is superfluous. Less is more. Let us thankfully accept this commentary about infinity as the utmost description of truth. Descriptions themselves are also superfluous for those getting a glimpse of the truth and experiencing "It" first-hand. This first-hand experience enabled Bodhidharma to report so authentically on his impressions.

Do not consider yourself to be separate from the path. In fact, you are one with it.

Perceive the fact that you are wandering. When there is no longer any goal or wanderer but only the wandering itself, this movement corresponds to what the Taoists call the Tao, a state which cannot be spoken, expressed, described or grasped, and which is actually unfathomable.

You will gradually realize that the Tao, the Oneness, the Divine, the Source, this "It" pervades you, whether you want it to or not. Our wanting and desiring are not indelibly linked with survival. Wanting is an ego process going against the flow of life. Struggling against the Tao is tiring and leads you nowhere! So, simply let go of the wanting, controlling and the wannabe. Let go and realize that you have played these games long enough. They have not gotten you any further, and have only made you unhappy.

The same applies to the spiritual path. Ultimately you will have to let go of doing and will have to relinquish control. You need to let go of the concepts so prevalent today of "achieving things on your own" and "through your own efforts." And you will have to surrender your attachment to the own self, which sees itself as separate from the Oneness.

Give up the idea that you as a separate individual can achieve spiritual progress. Do not cling to the fallacy that your actions can be the basis for enlightenment. Let go of the false belief that you are the one who is meditating. Yield to the Oneness and let it unfold what you are. Drop all the obstacles your ego throws on your path. Stop seeking and find the Self in your inner Being. Then you will "lock eyebrows" with the Masters and you will "know" what green tastes like.

Trust your inner resources to open the gates in you. This will enable you to "gain access" to the nameless. Then you will be ready to seek the core of your Being with meditation. You will be ready to create the necessary prerequisites.

Let us add a few words to the vast library of instructions

on, guides to and manuals on meditation. Perhaps one day Zen teachers will meet you in person at a meditation retreat or Sesshin (intensive Zen meditation). Perhaps we will be able at that moment to pass something from our hearts to yours. The only things that we have to teach are what we have experienced ourselves. The only way for you to understand them is with your heart!

Meditation brings you inner peace, grace and awareness to take you closer to the truth.

Practice makes perfect! So we have now come full circle. Perhaps you recall something mentioned at the beginning of this book: "When Being knows we call it meditation!" You have now arrived at the place where you always were to begin with. There is Nobody left who is seeking. There is no goal of "achieving" or "finding" anything, nor of having that single transformative or supernatural "experience" that many crave for, but of Being what you inherently are.

With your permission, we will point you in the right direction. It will be easier to persevere if you practice one of the methods more intensely, if you seek a teacher or Master or if you join a group of people who meditate. Group-dynamic processes activate the energy of all participants. This energy will help you get on the path to All-One. However, it does not matter whether you meditate by yourself or in a group. You are always All-One. This does not require any efforts on your part.

In any case, at this junction on the path, do not cling to the assumption that you have done anything for your spiritual development! This is simply not true!

However, if you do not practice, you will not give grace the opportunity to unfold in you.

There is a wide range of approaches to effectively calming

minds and to mindfully travel down the path of self-lessness. Without making any specific recommendations to you, these include Western concentration, shamanic techniques, chakra and sound meditations, mandalas, chanting holy syllables, yoga, pranayama (breathing) exercises, drumming, dancing, singing, crying, laughing, the martial arts, love in tantric meditation or sexual Kung-Fu, Qi Gong, Tai Chi, true praying, Zazen as well as many other techniques. These approaches engage your mind and thus keep it content, and do such without promoting restless activity.

Please note that people have always been fascinated with those who gain incredible psychic abilities, who supposedly are able to travel on other planes, who develop supernatural powers or who do spectacular feats with their bodies. Zen considers this to be a distraction and a misuse of our energies.

Please start out by placing your trust in what we say and assume that we are right when we say that meditation really does have positive effects. Should you not do this, you will not experience these effects. If you do not accept that such a method is capable of making you serene, empty and free, you will not devote yourself to it and you will not gain peace of mind. How do you expect to experience serenity if you cannot refrain from worrying, bothering and brooding about everything? How can you exist in a state of tranquility if you always seek to secure personal advantages for yourself and to prevent anything to your detriment?

When you let go, nothing else is of use to you any longer. This statement applies to all meditative approaches that enable you to completely be your-Self. Sitting down and only Being means just what it says: not having to do anything but sit and be.

All methods are tools that are at our disposal—and nothing more. These tools are not our goal. Nevertheless, we clarify things enough so that our minds know what is meant. It is recognizing what we long for, finding something "under all that garbage" and realizing a state of Being that has always existed.

Remember that the sun shines brightly even when it is hidden by the clouds and does not seem to be there.

Nobody is there who perceives. Nobody is left who strives, struggles and achieves. Nobody remains who sits down to meditate. This will be evident when you let go of your supposed ego and when the clouds shrouding the sun—namely the concepts, images and perceptions we have of ourselves—have disappeared.

"It." How can it be described? It cannot be grasped or comprehended, and it is not available to the one who still exists as a separate being, who still thinks she or he is a special someone. We are talking about someone who defines himself according to all the limitations of race, nationality, skin color, profession, gender, education and roles in life. We mean someone who still believes he is separate and detached from Existence and all sentient beings, a person who believes he has fallen out of the Oneness and been expelled from paradise. This person cannot enter.

Whoever understands that there is nothing to understand, whoever sees and realizes that there is no individual who is not bonded with everybody and everything, and who is not All-One, has found "It."

Whoever has cleared his mind and explored his spirit, who has permeated every corner of his being with mindfulness, and who does not find anything on his search and accepts this—the person is lifted up and thrives. He is now emptied and cleansed. He is Nobody and thus extraordinary.

The spirit that has lost nothing of what it was before now

delves deep into the nature of Existence, like dewdrops in the ocean. It is the ocean which pours into the dewdrops when the grace of Self-realization is there, to cite Kabir once more.

It is essential to realize that you have to lay down your life to retain it. If you have not realized it already: the seeker has been "found", with the realization that the seeker and that which was being sought are One. You are pure, clear consciousness. There is Nobody separating himself. Nor is there an individual who can be separate. You are universal Being or "Suchness" (which you always were) and have bonded with everything. You embody and flow through everything. There is Nobody cut off from Existence, upon whom wounds can be inflicted or scars can be left or who has to go somewhere. There is Nobody who needs to be "awakened" or "enlightened" because everyone already Is. Simply put, there is no seeker, nor anything to seek, but only the "Suchness" of Being.

There is only serenity and tranquility. There is deep peace at the moment when Nobody is left who can arrive somewhere. By laughing, you can realize that all the innate fears were unnecessary. It was never a question of "To be or not to be," to use one of the most famous questions ever uttered.[70]

Meditation will soon be an indispensable help on the pathless path, which as you know by now is not a path at all, and thus pathless. Seek to "get to the other side of the river" with a meditation technique you think is suitable for you. However, when you reach the other side, you will be able to push the boat back into the river because you will no longer need it. You will be carefree and happy.

In the Ten Ox Herding Pictures of Zen[71], those who are wise and who have overcome them-selves return to their normal activities in life. There is nothing that society or missionaries have to change. But a revolution has taken place in such people. They are now whole, intact, healed and holy. They breathe, exist and move in a state of equilibrium and harmony. They feel the divine greatness in themselves. It was always there and will always be there, and "It" is indestructible.

To be one with the usual things in life is extraordinarily unusual.

In order to be one with these things, you do not have to have extraordinary thoughts or do extraordinary things. You only have to be like the leaf on the river which loves the flow and its course in life. Whether you like it or not, "His will be done." Being takes place, and we are one with this spirit.

It was not necessary to learn anything, because the learner cannot get anything he has always had. It was not necessary for the teacher to instruct, because there is nothing that he could give. Nevertheless, we traveled a way along the path together. We now perceive more and more things, and do such without being enthralled and spellbound by them!

By going forth without moving and flowing without stopping, our legs never moved, and the path did not move.

The spirit moved in and through us!

ABOUT THE EGO

This is related in deep veneration of the great Zen Master Kyozan Joshu Sasaki Roshi (born 1907), bowing down with humility in the Zen gassho and sampai positions. He stated:

"You have to give up the ego. You can only claim to have studied Zen when you have realized the origins of God, Buddha and people. Shakyamuni[72] said the origin of everything is emptiness."

Emptiness or nothingness is the source itself, therefore free of everything and encompassing everything. God, or Buddha, has no form, no color and no voice. It is exactly the same with your own true Self. When you are based in the ego, you fear God and evil. You believe a pretty woman is attractive and an ugly woman not attractive. This is not your true Self.

Your true Self is free of beauty and ugliness, free of God and evil. You are free of everything at the moment in which you manifest as emptiness.

BRING US YOUR CHAINS

I MAGINE YOU COULD be a pebble letting itself fall into the river and thus letting go of everything. As such, you look at all beings with compassion. Whatever you see shows you the presence of God. You see the Oneness in everything. Whenever you see someone, you see the Buddha. Every action of yours is sacred and carried out with mindfulness. You know that you are at home in the here-now. This is the vision so eloquently depicted by the Buddhist monk Thich Nhat Hanh.

However, for most of us, living in this manner cannot be achieved by snapping our fingers or by exerting willpower. We have to contend with all of the garbage, obstacles, explanations and threats that the ego process comes up with. We always carry Gollum around with us. This is akin to Frodo's quest, to his struggles and his almost succumbing to the ring's powers. Frodo finally manages to throw the ring into Mount Doom and thus get rid of it once and for all. His success is thanks to grace or divine intervention, or perhaps a fortunate accident.[73]

Whoever said life was easy? Buddha told us that our existence is indelibly linked with suffering. Pain, illness and the death of our physical bodies are preprogrammed. We are often confronted with so many things that "push our buttons," demand our attention and sap our energy. We are constantly faced with "threatening" news and events, and must deal with the necessity of earning a living, raising a family and much more. Life remains an incredible challenge, notwithstanding all of the amenities of modern life many of us enjoy.

However, even if this book has not managed to answer every single question you have, it has hopefully awakened you to the existence of the pathless path you have always been on. Going down this path will enable you to deal with suffering, to overcome the bondage of your ego processes, to gain serenity and inner peace and to enjoy life more.

Most importantly: grace enables you to embrace the infinite Self, to abide in the Oneness and to BE what you really are—to be "authentic"—even in the light of all our "mistakes," imperfections, the limitations imposed by the body and mind and whatever happens to us. Our core—our dignity—is inviolable! The pathless path enables you to open yourself up and create the space for the Divine to enter. That is the real game-changer. You will see that you ultimately cannot hide, deny, disown, suppress or resist the real you.

Buddha asked us to work diligently for our own salvation. Osho tells us that Buddha's last words were "Sammasati"— "Remember that you are a Buddha."[74] The transition to a mindful, blissful life, from self-importance to self-lessness, may not be easy and does definitely require time and commitment.[75] But it is worth the effort.

There are innumerable books available on how to meditate, practice mindfulness, and live in the here-now. They explain what Zen is all about. If you want to go down the path of meditation, then thoroughly acquaint yourself with it, its training and techniques. Set a date for selecting a type of meditation. Find out which one is suitable and practical for you, and then really practice it.

Personally, we recommend Zazen and its practice of meditation without a purpose. In such practices, one lets

Bring Us Your Chains

thoughts and images pass by like clouds in the sky. One does not fight against them. One focuses on breathing and Being. Zazen was the approach taken by Buddha, and reflects what this book is saying. Meditation is designed to help you BE what you already are: a pure, unconditional, Absolute Being. No goal is involved. This makes meditation unintentional.

In our work, we often encounter people who are searching. Their searches are often for the most optimal form of meditation—instead of for their original Being and inherent nature. As a result, our sessions become another way to keep these people busy and to distract them from focusing on the essentials.

Returning to the center and to the core of your inner Being does not mean that you relinquish your interest in external things. Instead, it means that you realize inside of you that originally everything is good.

Liberation, realization, enlightenment—whatever term you choose to use—are only necessary in our minds, in which we falsely cling to the concept of seeing ourselves and Existence as being separate.

However, even if you do not realize this, you are still who you are, who you have always been and will always be, because your true identity is independent of realization, unintentional and timeless. You are pure Being.

You can rediscover yourself again as being free from suffering and as never having been lost.

We sincerely thank all the many people who have accompanied and supported us, all the Masters and other great ones, for having inspired us and having shown us the pathless path. We also thank all sentient beings, and bow down to the Oneness in them.

We ask you, the wanderer who has accompanied us so far

on the pathless path, to please understand that there is no need to differentiate between good and evil, black and white. There is no need to make distinctions based on sexual, religious and political identities. We are all bonded in the one Spirit, the Oneness.

You are the Self, originally unintentional undividedness. There is only the Self!

That which tries to separate and alienate you was only an idea in your mind, which took the place of your true state of Being. By recognizing the vast, open expanses of the Oneness and the undivided Spirit, you realize that suffering is a door to go through.

The pathless path seamlessly leads to the gateless gates. Realizing both is everything, because both are ultimately nothing. "Form is emptiness and emptiness is form"—and you are now in the midst of Self-realization.

No one can say anything about this without missing the point. But who has to say anything?

Do you still feel that you are imprisoned? Do you still think that you are enchained? Do you still think that you have not yet been freed?

An instructive story is told about Huike and his encounter with Bodhidharma, the founder of Chan. Huike said to him "My mind is not yet at peace; please pacify it for me."

Bodhidharma said, "Bring me your mind and I will pacify it for you."

After years of searching, Huike said to Bodhidharma, "I have looked for my mind. I cannot find it."

Bodhidharma said, "Then I have pacified your mind for you."

Bring us your chains!

AFTERWORD

by Xue Feng

F<small>IND THE</small> S<small>EEKER</small>!
... is a message of happiness, being successful and being a success oneself.

The Tathagata (historical Buddha) neither established teachings, a school or even Buddhism! He only spoke of the stillness of truth. In his day and age, there were no "-isms" or "-ists" and thus no Buddh-ism or Buddh-ists. There was only the practice of Buddhadharma.

Generations after Tathagata, his instructions were put down in writing and encompassed in a canon, which dogmatized and institutionalized truth. Various schools, sects and traditions arose as part of what we call Buddhism. Even Chan Buddhism (which emerged in China) was not spared, and became a dogmatic system of theories. It is even classified as a sect or school.

The vibrancy of Buddhadharma became a dead form of worship and idol worship, as an instrument of power for strength and a pacifier for weakness, as a sound of illusion considered to be the truth.

There are almost only preachers and believers, in which case the believer walks down the path of experience taken by others, attached to dogmas without striving for the experience himself. He rests on a spiritual hammock, sucks the "finger that points to the moon," bathes in the atmosphere of nebulous, blurry mysticism, or plays with an intellectual baby rattle which he calls knowledge. Because it is far from true practice, he clings to fundamentalism and the authority of the "Word." If Buddhadharma does not correspond to one's own shortcomings, it is bent into shape and mixed with an esoteric porridge. The patchwork down turns into a cozy, feel-good patchwork blanket to shield him from the truth.

Some even smugly called themselves Chan Masters, wading like a stork in salad through a multitude of submissive admirers and devotees. However, they are basically gravediggers and adorers of the Buddhadharma and a servant of Mara.

In their midst, Buddhas and patriarchs in their patchwork gowns wander, ready to accompany serious seekers. Whoever finds their way to them is immediately confronted with the principle, "Learn or clear off!" They do not feed but take away the food! They do not stand on the graves of their predecessors, are independent of ideologies, do not play with a spiritual baby rattle, are free of intellectual trends, stay away from fundamentalist complaining and reject the sentimental group mentality.

These Buddhas and patriarchs are guides to the "Gateless Gate" of Dharma, and guardians of the "Gateless Gate," so that only people without rank and name can pass through.

For them, there is only working to attain freedom and relieve suffering! Whoever knows suffering and does not want to continue suffering needs neither Chan practice nor can he pass through the gate. It is simple: whoever does not take time to abolish suffering has to take time to suffer.

Chan is the audacity of thinking against traditions. To be

a Chan practitioner means to be a heretic, even against Chan itself.

Such a person is my friend and brother in Dharma, Genro Laoshi. We are neither Chan teachers nor Chan Masters! Genro is a guide, nothing more and nothing less. With his book, "Find the Seeker!," he touches your heart and poses the question, "Who are you wanderer, full of craving for true Zen?"

—Xue Feng,
Abbot of the Ding Shan Monastery,
brother in Dharma of Genro Laoshi and Chan Master named by Abbot Shi Chan Ming.
Xue Feng is also Konrad von Moresbach of the Oblates of the Order of St. Benedict.

ABOUT THE AUTHORS

Gert G. Beirer, who was born in Austria in 1945, studied Zen, meditation, Kung-Fu, Qi Gong and acupuncture in Asia, and works as a senior business consultant, university lecturer and therapist. He was given the name Genro ("Origin of Joy") Xuan Lou, Laoshi (Laoshi = "Spiritual Master") by Zen Master Tetsuo Kiichi Nagaya Roshi. Genro Xuan Lou, Laoshi was named Zen (Chan) Master by the Abbot and Grand Master Kun Kong at the Lingyin Temple (Shakyamuni Buddhism) in Hangzhou, with whom he studied eleven years, by Abbot and Zen Master Shi Chan Ming in Wuhan, Province Hubei, China, and was also named Shifu or "Spiritual Teacher" in 2009 by Shi Xue Feng, Abbot of the Ding Shan Temple in Germany.

Clifford Stevens (Ki-ichi) was born in the United States. His career included stints as a teacher, journalist, PR manager and translator. He has studied Qi Gong, Zen and meditation under Genro Xuan Lou, Laoshi for many years. His meditation-imparted experiences and the Dharma transmission from Genro have qualified him to be a teacher of Zen. He humbly reveals his deep insights and awareness of the spiritual cosmos as he wanders along the pathless path with his Zen Master.

With their eyebrows locked, Genro and Ki-ichi joined to write this book in the One Spirit, which is unique in the world of Zen.

ADDITIONAL READING

WE HOPE THIS book has inspired you to turn within and to make your way down the pathless path. Our objective has not been to provide your minds with even more matters to ponder, but on unfolding what you already are.

Notwithstanding this, there are a large number of books on spirituality that could serve as signposts on your path to knowledge. Below is a selection of the writers that we find to be inspiring and beneficial.

These works include such masterpieces as Lao Tzu (*Tao de Ching*), Joshu (*The Recorded Sayings of Zen Master Joshu*), and the *I Ching* or *Book of Changes* (in the translation by Richard Wilhelm). Other longstanding favorites include such collections as *Zen Flesh, Zen Bones: A Collection of Zen and Pre-Zen Writings,* edited by Paul Reps; John Blofield's *The Zen Teachings of Huang Po*; *Treasury of the True Dharma Eye: Zen Master Dogen's Shobo Genzo*, edited by Kazuaki Tanahashi. Also to be recommended are books on Huineng and Meister Eckhart.

Contemporary writers include the Dalai Lama (*How to Practice: The Way to a Meaningful Life, How to See Yourself as You Really Are*), Eckhart Tolle (*The Power of Now*), Thich Nhat Hanh (*Peace is Every Step, You Are Here*), David Steindl-Rast

(*Fullness and Emptiness, Music of Silence: A Sacred Journey Through the Hours of the Day*), Wolfgang Kopp (*Free Yourself of Everything, Zen Beyond All Words*), Osho (*The Book of Understanding, The Zen Manifesto: Freedom From Oneself*), Sri Nisargadatta Maharaj (*I AM THAT: Talks With Sri Sri Nisargadatta Maharaj*), Taizen Deshimaru-Roshi (*Sit: Zen Teachings of Master Taizen Deshimaru*), Shunryu Suzuki (*Zen Mind, Beginner's Mind*), Sri Ramana Maharshi (*Be As You Are*), Seung Sahn (*The Compass of Zen*), Joel Goldsmith (*The Infinite Way*), Virginia Stephenson (*The Healing Christ Love*), Bhante Henpola Gunaratana (*Mindfulness in Plain English*), Mantak Chia (*Iron Shirt Chi Kung"*), Paul Coelho (*Warrior of the Light*), Anthony de Mello (*Awareness*), Tony Parsons (*As It Is: The Open Secret to Living an Awakened Life*), Tai Sheridan (*Buddha in Blue Jeans: An Extremely Short Zen Guide to Sitting Quietly and Being Buddha*), Barry Magid (*Ending the Pursuit of Happiness: A Zen Guide*), Robert Rosenbaum (*Walking the Way: 81 Zen Encounters with the Tao Te Ching*), John Tarrant (*The Light Inside the Dark: Zen, Soul and the Spiritual Life*), Tim Burkett (*Nothing Holy About It: The Zen of Being Just Who You Are*) and Enza Vita (*Instance Presence: Allow Natural Meditation to Happen*).

For poetic inspiration, turn to Rumi (e.g. *The Book of Love, Poems of Ecstasy and Longing*), Kabir (e.g. *The Poetry of Kabir*) or Rabindranath Tagore (e.g. *Gitanjali*) to give just a few examples.

NOTES

1. An ancient Chinese text considered to be influential in adapting Buddhism and Taoism to Chinese culture. The Masters quoted in this book are freely translated.
2. Matthew: 7:7-8
3. *I AM THAT: Talks with Sri Nisargadatta Maharaj*
4. Eckhart Tolle, *The Power of Now, Practicing the Power of Now*
5. 1868-1912.
6. The first Chinese Patriarch, Bodhidharma, a Buddhist monk said to have brought Dhyana from India to China, is often referred to simply as Dharma, or Ta-Mo in Chinese. Dhyana in Japan became known as "Zen", and in China as "Ch'an or Chan). The words of Ta-Mo go back to the texts of Tun-Huang in China and are taken from various translations.
7. Osho, *The Book of Understanding.*
8. Store consciousness or root consciousness is where our past experiences are stored, which Western psychology refers to as the unconscious mind.
9. According to the Book of Genesis in the Old Testament, Adam and Eve disobeyed God and ate the fruit from the

Tree of Knowledge, also known as the tree of knowledge of good and evil. This is the Original Sin.

10 Original Face refers to the non-dual Buddha nature. The Zen koan can be freely translated as "What was your original face before your father and mother were born?"

11 A koan is a paradoxical puzzle, mystery or statement designed to get people to abandon their dependence on logic and reason.

12 Visualizing a large glowing ball of energy or light is often used in healing, relaxation and centering exercises.

13 For comprehension purposes, the forms "he" and "him" are generally used in this book to refer to an individual. However, no assumptions are made here about gender identity nor is any offense intended.

14 The 10,000 Things refer to all phenomenal reality, as described in the *Tao Te Ching* of Lao Tzu.

15 Exodus 3:14.

16 To lock eyebrows with the Masters is to join together with them in the Oneness, in realizing your true Self.

17 A fictional place in the novel *Lost Horizon* written by James Hilton.

18 A statement by Zen monk and teacher Issan Dorsey Roshi.

19 Matthew 10:39.

20 In the film *The Matrix*, the spoon exists in the Matrix but not in reality. In other words, you cannot change the spoon as a supposed part of reality, but the perception of reality.

21 Hui Neng was a Master of Chan Buddhism born in the year 638.

22 Matthew 16:25.
23 Goethe, The Holy Longing, a poem translated by Robert Bly.
24 For example Luke 22:42.
25 Namaste is a Hindu greeting, meaning the spirit (or divine light) in me bows to the spirit in you.
26 Posa is one of the characters in Verdi's opera, *Don Carlos*.
27 From the "Heart Sutra", one of the most popular Buddhist scriptures. It is part of the Prajnaparamita Sutra, and is a teaching by the Bodhisattva Avalokitesvara, the Buddha of Compassion, to the monk Shariputra.
28 From the Gateless Gate, "Not the wind, not the flag". Two monks were arguing. One said the flag was moving, the other said the wind was moving. The patriarch overheard this and said, "Not the wind, not the flag, mind is moving". There is nothing outside of the One Consciousness.
29 John 8:58.
30 Indian mystic and poet from the 14th or 15th century.
31 The iron flute, a type of flute without holes or a mouthpiece to blow, symbolizes the vain attempts of people to understand the inherent mysteries of life using logic.
32 The Last Things commonly refer to death, judgment, heaven and hell.
33 Lao Tzu, *Tao de Ching*.
34 Exodus 20:4.
35 Moloch was originally a pagan fire god demanding child sacrifice, and was later seen as one of Satan's angels.
36 Master Yaoshan was a Zen Buddhist monk during the

Tang dynasty. It is quoted in the book *Treasury of the True Dharma Eye: Zen Master Dogen's Shobo Genzo*.

37 Matthew 18:3.
38 Jesus said, "I am the way, the truth and the life". John 14:6.
39 John 17:14.
40 Exodus 3:14.
41 Matthew 8:22.
42 "The Great Way has no gate,/A thousand roads enter it./ When one passes through this gateless gate,/He freely walks between heaven and earth." This Zen Buddhist poem by Wumen Huikai is in a preface to a book of koans, and "The Great Way" is the path to enlightenment.
43 John 18:6.
44 The dragon is a symbol of heavenly creativity and strength.
45 Attributed to Austrian artist Friedensreich Hundertwasser.
46 Alexander is said to have stated: "I want people to know that I came empty handed into this world and likewise will go empty handed from this world."
47 Johann Wolfgang von Goethe, Faust, Part I.
48 Indra's net, the net cast by the Vedic god Indra, symbolizes the interconnectedness of the Universe as well as non-duality.
49 An anonymous work of Christian mysticism, dated at the end of the 14th century.
50 Plato, Cratylus, 402a.
51 The great Taoist from the 4th century B.C.
52 William Shakespeare *The Tempest*.

Notes

53 "The Serenity Prayer" by Reinhold Niebuhr, an American theologian.

54 The Greek philosopher Aristotle.

55 This analogy is by the American spiritual teacher Ram Dass, author of the book *Be Here Now*.

56 Attributed to Zen Master Yun Men who lived in the 10th century.

57 Matthew 5-7.

58 Matthew 5:3.

59 John 17: 14-16

60 In the Sermon on the Mount, Jesus admonished us not to believe we could serve two masters—both God and money.

61 Bearing false witness is a grave offense according to the Ninth Commandment in the Old Testament.

62 The Hindu deity Shiva, one of the three members of the triumvirate along with Brahma and Vishnu, is known as the destroyer or transformer.

63 His books include *Peace is Every Step*, *You Are Here*, *The Miracle of Mindfulness*.

64 *The Teachings of Sri Ramana Maharshi*, edited by David Godman.

65 Marcus Aurelius, *Meditations*.

66 The Persian mystic and poet Rumi wrote in his work *Inner Wakefulness*: There is an inner wakefulness that directs the dream and that will eventually startle us back to the truth of who we are.

67 Author of the book of poems entitled *Gitanjali*(Song Offerings) and winner of the Nobel Prize for Literature.

68 Taken from the famous prayer popularly known as "St. Teresa's Bookmark" from Teresa of Avila, 16th century Carmelite nun and mystic and later named as a saint.
69 Joel Goldsmith, *The Infinite Way*.
70 Posed by Prince Hamlet in William Shakespeare's play *Hamlet*.
71 The Zen Ox Herding Pictures are images designed to illustrate progress made towards enlightenment and returning to the One Source. They probably originated in the 12th century.
72 Gautama Siddhartha, the historical Buddha, who lived some 2,500 years ago.
73 J.R.R. Tolkien, *The Lord of the Rings*.
74 Osho, *Discover the Buddha*.
75 Osho, *The Zen Manifesto, Freedom from Oneself*.

Please visit us at:
www.findtheseeker.com

Printed by BoD™in Norderstedt, Germany